50% OFF Online NCE Prep Course!

Dear Customer,

We consider it an honor and a privilege that you chose our NCE Study Guide. As a way of showing our appreciation and to help us better serve you, we have partnered with Mometrix Test Preparation to offer **50% off their online NCE Prep Course**. Many NCE courses are needlessly expensive and don't deliver enough value. With our course, you get access to the best NCE prep material, and you only pay half price.

Mometrix has structured their online course to perfectly complement your printed study guide. The NCE Prep Course contains **over 40 lessons** that cover all the most important topics, **20+ video reviews** that explain difficult concepts, **over 1,000 practice questions** to ensure you feel prepared, and **over 450 digital flashcards**, so you can study while you're on the go.

Online NCE Prep Course

Topics Covered:	*Course Features:*
• Human Growth and Development	• NCE Study Guide
• Fundamentals of Counseling	o Get content that complements our best-selling study guide.
• Assessment and Testing	
• Social and Cultural Diversity	• 5 Full-Length Practice Tests
• Counseling and Helping Relationships	o With over 1,000 practice questions, you can test yourself again and again.
• Group Counseling and Group Work	
• Career Development	• Mobile Friendly
• Professional Counseling Orientation and Ethical Practice	o If you need to study on the go, the course is easily accessible from your mobile device.
• Research and Program Evaluation	
	• NCE Flashcards
	o Their course includes a flashcard mode consisting of over 450 content cards to help you study.

To receive this discount, visit their website: https://www.mometrix.com/university/courses/nce and add the course to your cart. At the checkout page, enter the discount code: **TPBNCE50**

If you have any questions or concerns, please don't hesitate to contact them at universityhelp@mometrix.com.

Sincerely,

FREE Test Taking Tips DVD Offer

To help us better serve you, we have developed a Test Taking Tips DVD that we would like to give you for FREE. **This DVD covers world-class test taking tips that you can use to be even more successful when you are taking your test.**

All that we ask is that you email us your feedback about your study guide. Please let us know what you thought about it – whether that is good, bad or indifferent.

To get your **FREE Test Taking Tips DVD**, email freedvd@studyguideteam.com with "FREE DVD" in the subject line and the following information in the body of the email:

    a. The title of your study guide.

    b. Your product rating on a scale of 1-5, with 5 being the highest rating.

    c. Your feedback about the study guide. What did you think of it?

    d. Your full name and shipping address to send your free DVD.

If you have any questions or concerns, please don't hesitate to contact us at freedvd@studyguideteam.com.

Thanks again!

NCE Exam Preparation Study Guide

NCE Exam Prep and Practice Test Questions
[3rd Edition]

TPB Publishing

Written and edited by TPB Publishing

TPB Publishing is not associated with or endorsed by any official testing organization. TPB Publishing is a publisher of unofficial educational products. All test and organization names are trademarks of their respective owners. Content in this book is included for utilitarian purposes only and does not constitute an endorsement by TPB Publishing of any particular point of view.

Interested in buying more than 10 copies of our product? Contact us about bulk discounts:
bulkorders@studyguideteam.com

ISBN 13: 9781628458619
ISBN 10: 1628458615

Table of Contents

Quick Overview

As you draw closer to taking your exam, effective preparation becomes more and more important. Thankfully, you have this study guide to help you get ready. Use this guide to help keep your studying on track and refer to it often.

This study guide contains several key sections that will help you be successful on your exam. The guide contains tips for what you should do the night before and the day of the test. Also included are test-taking tips. Knowing the right information is not always enough. Many well-prepared test takers struggle with exams. These tips will help equip you to accurately read, assess, and answer test questions.

A large part of the guide is devoted to showing you what content to expect on the exam and to helping you better understand that content. In this guide are practice test questions so that you can see how well you have grasped the content. Then, answer explanations are provided so that you can understand why you missed certain questions.

Don't try to cram the night before you take your exam. This is not a wise strategy for a few reasons. First, your retention of the information will be low. Your time would be better used by reviewing information you already know rather than trying to learn a lot of new information. Second, you will likely become stressed as you try to gain a large amount of knowledge in a short amount of time. Third, you will be depriving yourself of sleep. So be sure to go to bed at a reasonable time the night before. Being well-rested helps you focus and remain calm.

Be sure to eat a substantial breakfast the morning of the exam. If you are taking the exam in the afternoon, be sure to have a good lunch as well. Being hungry is distracting and can make it difficult to focus. You have hopefully spent lots of time preparing for the exam. Don't let an empty stomach get in the way of success!

When travelling to the testing center, leave earlier than needed. That way, you have a buffer in case you experience any delays. This will help you remain calm and will keep you from missing your appointment time at the testing center.

Be sure to pace yourself during the exam. Don't try to rush through the exam. There is no need to risk performing poorly on the exam just so you can leave the testing center early. Allow yourself to use all of the allotted time if needed.

Remain positive while taking the exam even if you feel like you are performing poorly. Thinking about the content you should have mastered will not help you perform better on the exam.

Once the exam is complete, take some time to relax. Even if you feel that you need to take the exam again, you will be well served by some down time before you begin studying again. It's often easier to convince yourself to study if you know that it will come with a reward!

Test-Taking Strategies

1. Predicting the Answer

When you feel confident in your preparation for a multiple-choice test, try predicting the answer before reading the answer choices. This is especially useful on questions that test objective factual knowledge. By predicting the answer before reading the available choices, you eliminate the possibility that you will be distracted or led astray by an incorrect answer choice. You will feel more confident in your selection if you read the question, predict the answer, and then find your prediction among the answer choices. After using this strategy, be sure to still read all of the answer choices carefully and completely. If you feel unprepared, you should not attempt to predict the answers. This would be a waste of time and an opportunity for your mind to wander in the wrong direction.

2. Reading the Whole Question

Too often, test takers scan a multiple-choice question, recognize a few familiar words, and immediately jump to the answer choices. Test authors are aware of this common impatience, and they will sometimes prey upon it. For instance, a test author might subtly turn the question into a negative, or he or she might redirect the focus of the question right at the end. The only way to avoid falling into these traps is to read the entirety of the question carefully before reading the answer choices.

3. Looking for Wrong Answers

Long and complicated multiple-choice questions can be intimidating. One way to simplify a difficult multiple-choice question is to eliminate all of the answer choices that are clearly wrong. In most sets of answers, there will be at least one selection that can be dismissed right away. If the test is administered on paper, the test taker could draw a line through it to indicate that it may be ignored; otherwise, the test taker will have to perform this operation mentally or on scratch paper. In either case, once the obviously incorrect answers have been eliminated, the remaining choices may be considered. Sometimes identifying the clearly wrong answers will give the test taker some information about the correct answer. For instance, if one of the remaining answer choices is a direct opposite of one of the eliminated answer choices, it may well be the correct answer. The opposite of obviously wrong is obviously right! Of course, this is not always the case. Some answers are obviously incorrect simply because they are irrelevant to the question being asked. Still, identifying and eliminating some incorrect answer choices is a good way to simplify a multiple-choice question.

4. Don't Overanalyze

Anxious test takers often overanalyze questions. When you are nervous, your brain will often run wild, causing you to make associations and discover clues that don't actually exist. If you feel that this may be a problem for you, do whatever you can to slow down during the test. Try taking a deep breath or counting to ten. As you read and consider the question, restrict yourself to the particular words used by the author. Avoid thought tangents about what the author *really* meant, or what he or she was *trying* to say. The only things that matter on a multiple-choice test are the words that are actually in the question. You must avoid reading too much into a multiple-choice question, or supposing that the writer meant something other than what he or she wrote.

5. No Need for Panic

It is wise to learn as many strategies as possible before taking a multiple-choice test, but it is likely that you will come across a few questions for which you simply don't know the answer. In this situation, avoid panicking. Because most multiple-choice tests include dozens of questions, the relative value of a single wrong answer is small. As much as possible, you should compartmentalize each question on a multiple-choice test. In other words, you should not allow your feelings about one question to affect your success on the others. When you find a question that you either don't understand or don't know how to answer, just take a deep breath and do your best. Read the entire question slowly and carefully. Try rephrasing the question a couple of different ways. Then, read all of the answer choices carefully. After eliminating obviously wrong answers, make a selection and move on to the next question.

6. Confusing Answer Choices

When working on a difficult multiple-choice question, there may be a tendency to focus on the answer choices that are the easiest to understand. Many people, whether consciously or not, gravitate to the answer choices that require the least concentration, knowledge, and memory. This is a mistake. When you come across an answer choice that is confusing, you should give it extra attention. A question might be confusing because you do not know the subject matter to which it refers. If this is the case, don't eliminate the answer before you have affirmatively settled on another. When you come across an answer choice of this type, set it aside as you look at the remaining choices. If you can confidently assert that one of the other choices is correct, you can leave the confusing answer aside. Otherwise, you will need to take a moment to try to better understand the confusing answer choice. Rephrasing is one way to tease out the sense of a confusing answer choice.

7. Your First Instinct

Many people struggle with multiple-choice tests because they overthink the questions. If you have studied sufficiently for the test, you should be prepared to trust your first instinct once you have carefully and completely read the question and all of the answer choices. There is a great deal of research suggesting that the mind can come to the correct conclusion very quickly once it has obtained all of the relevant information. At times, it may seem to you as if your intuition is working faster even than your reasoning mind. This may in fact be true. The knowledge you obtain while studying may be retrieved from your subconscious before you have a chance to work out the associations that support it. Verify your instinct by working out the reasons that it should be trusted.

8. Key Words

Many test takers struggle with multiple-choice questions because they have poor reading comprehension skills. Quickly reading and understanding a multiple-choice question requires a mixture of skill and experience. To help with this, try jotting down a few key words and phrases on a piece of scrap paper. Doing this concentrates the process of reading and forces the mind to weigh the relative importance of the question's parts. In selecting words and phrases to write down, the test taker thinks about the question more deeply and carefully. This is especially true for multiple-choice questions that are preceded by a long prompt.

9. Subtle Negatives

One of the oldest tricks in the multiple-choice test writer's book is to subtly reverse the meaning of a question with a word like *not* or *except*. If you are not paying attention to each word in the question, you can easily be led astray by this trick. For instance, a common question format is, "Which of the following is...?" Obviously, if the question instead is, "Which of the following is not...?," then the answer will be quite different. Even worse, the test makers are aware of the potential for this mistake and will include one answer choice that would be correct if the question were not negated or reversed. A test taker who misses the reversal will find what he or she believes to be a correct answer and will be so confident that he or she will fail to reread the question and discover the original error. The only way to avoid this is to practice a wide variety of multiple-choice questions and to pay close attention to each and every word.

10. Reading Every Answer Choice

It may seem obvious, but you should always read every one of the answer choices! Too many test takers fall into the habit of scanning the question and assuming that they understand the question because they recognize a few key words. From there, they pick the first answer choice that answers the question they believe they have read. Test takers who read all of the answer choices might discover that one of the latter answer choices is actually *more* correct. Moreover, reading all of the answer choices can remind you of facts related to the question that can help you arrive at the correct answer. Sometimes, a misstatement or incorrect detail in one of the latter answer choices will trigger your memory of the subject and will enable you to find the right answer. Failing to read all of the answer choices is like not reading all of the items on a restaurant menu: you might miss out on the perfect choice.

11. Spot the Hedges

One of the keys to success on multiple-choice tests is paying close attention to every word. This is never truer than with words like almost, most, some, and sometimes. These words are called "hedges" because they indicate that a statement is not totally true or not true in every place and time. An absolute statement will contain no hedges, but in many subjects, the answers are not always straightforward or absolute. There are always exceptions to the rules in these subjects. For this reason, you should favor those multiple-choice questions that contain hedging language. The presence of qualifying words indicates that the author is taking special care with his or her words, which is certainly important when composing the right answer. After all, there are many ways to be wrong, but there is only one way to be right! For this reason, it is wise to avoid answers that are absolute when taking a multiple-choice test. An absolute answer is one that says things are either all one way or all another. They often include words like *every*, *always*, *best*, and *never*. If you are taking a multiple-choice test in a subject that doesn't lend itself to absolute answers, be on your guard if you see any of these words.

12. Long Answers

In many subject areas, the answers are not simple. As already mentioned, the right answer often requires hedges. Another common feature of the answers to a complex or subjective question are qualifying clauses, which are groups of words that subtly modify the meaning of the sentence. If the question or answer choice describes a rule to which there are exceptions or the subject matter is complicated, ambiguous, or confusing, the correct answer will require many words in order to be expressed clearly and accurately. In essence, you should not be deterred by answer choices that seem excessively long. Oftentimes, the author of the text will not be able to write the correct answer without

offering some qualifications and modifications. Your job is to read the answer choices thoroughly and completely and to select the one that most accurately and precisely answers the question.

13. Restating to Understand

Sometimes, a question on a multiple-choice test is difficult not because of what it asks but because of how it is written. If this is the case, restate the question or answer choice in different words. This process serves a couple of important purposes. First, it forces you to concentrate on the core of the question. In order to rephrase the question accurately, you have to understand it well. Rephrasing the question will concentrate your mind on the key words and ideas. Second, it will present the information to your mind in a fresh way. This process may trigger your memory and render some useful scrap of information picked up while studying.

14. True Statements

Sometimes an answer choice will be true in itself, but it does not answer the question. This is one of the main reasons why it is essential to read the question carefully and completely before proceeding to the answer choices. Too often, test takers skip ahead to the answer choices and look for true statements. Having found one of these, they are content to select it without reference to the question above. Obviously, this provides an easy way for test makers to play tricks. The savvy test taker will always read the entire question before turning to the answer choices. Then, having settled on a correct answer choice, he or she will refer to the original question and ensure that the selected answer is relevant. The mistake of choosing a correct-but-irrelevant answer choice is especially common on questions related to specific pieces of objective knowledge. A prepared test taker will have a wealth of factual knowledge at his or her disposal, and should not be careless in its application.

15. No Patterns

One of the more dangerous ideas that circulates about multiple-choice tests is that the correct answers tend to fall into patterns. These erroneous ideas range from a belief that B and C are the most common right answers, to the idea that an unprepared test-taker should answer "A-B-A-C-A-D-A-B-A." It cannot be emphasized enough that pattern-seeking of this type is exactly the WRONG way to approach a multiple-choice test. To begin with, it is highly unlikely that the test maker will plot the correct answers according to some predetermined pattern. The questions are scrambled and delivered in a random order. Furthermore, even if the test maker was following a pattern in the assignation of correct answers, there is no reason why the test taker would know which pattern he or she was using. Any attempt to discern a pattern in the answer choices is a waste of time and a distraction from the real work of taking the test. A test taker would be much better served by extra preparation before the test than by reliance on a pattern in the answers.

FREE DVD OFFER

Don't forget that doing well on your exam includes both understanding the test content and understanding how to use what you know to do well on the test. We offer a completely FREE Test Taking Tips DVD that covers world class test taking tips that you can use to be even more successful when you are taking your test.

All that we ask is that you email us your feedback about your study guide. To get your **FREE Test Taking Tips DVD**, email freedvd@studyguideteam.com with "FREE DVD" in the subject line and the following information in the body of the email:

- The title of your study guide.
- Your product rating on a scale of 1-5, with 5 being the highest rating.
- Your feedback about the study guide. What did you think of it?
- Your full name and shipping address to send your free DVD.

Introduction to the NCE

Function of the Test

The National Counselor Examination for Licensure and Certification (NCE) is used in many states as well as military health systems. This test is a requirement for National Certified Counselor (NCC) certification. The test was first introduced in 1983 and is reviewed regularly to ensure validity and new research, and reflects current practices in counseling. This test is for recent college graduates hoping to become certified as counselors and is also used by professional counselors wishing to gain national certification.

The National Board for Certified Counselors (NBCC) has now credentialed counselors in over forty countries. Now over 40,000 counselors have received national counselor certification. In 2012, approximately 2,680 tests were given and 2,243 tests with passing scores were earned. The NBCC is internationally recognized for counselor certification exams. All fifty states, including Puerto Rico and District of Columbia, administer these tests.

The NBCC has a reputation of excellence. The NBCC and its affiliate, the Center for Credentialing and Education (CCE), oversee examination processes across the United States and abroad.

Test Administration

To reserve a seat for the NCE, an individual must fill out an application form and include a sealed college transcript. The transcript must verify a degree in counseling or related field. The test will begin at 9am and will last no longer than four hours. The test may be written or computer based—an individual will need to check with local agencies for verification. If special accommodations are required, they should be requested when submitting the registration. The candidate handbook contains guidelines and documentation requirements when submitting a request for special accommodations. The request will be reviewed for approval by the National Board for Certified Counselors (NBCC).

Retesting can be done after a three-month waiting period; another test fee will be required. Testing is typically during the first two full weeks of each month. Although application forms may be submitted any time, it is advised to submit paperwork sixty days prior to a desired exam time. States differ in what additional tests may need to be taken for state licensure in counseling. Therefore, taking and passing the NCE does not automatically qualify an individual for certification. An individual must check with their state to identify if any other tests are required for certification.

Test Format

The National Counselors Examination is divided into eight categories: Human Growth and Development, Social and Cultural Diversity, Helping Relationships, Group Work, Career Development, Assessment, Research and Program Evaluation, and Professional Orientation and Ethical Practice. There are 160 questions and 40 pretest questions.

The chart below outlines the areas of the NCE test and the number of questions for each.

NCE Test Subject Areas	# of Questions
Human Growth and Development	12
Social and Cultural Diversity	11
Helping Relationships	36
Group Work	16
Career Development	20
Assessment	20
Research and Program Evaluation	16
Professional Orientation and Ethical Practice	29
Total	**160**

These categories and test questions will be based off of five areas: Fundamentals of Counseling, Assessment/Career Counseling, Group Counseling, Programmatic and Clinical Intervention, and Professional Practice Issues.

Scoring

Experts in the counseling field review the test to decide on a passing score. Results will be received by mail within two months of the test date. Score reports will contain the number of correct responses with the total score, the mean and standard deviation for the testing period, and the minimum passing score. The maximum score a candidate can achieve is 160. If a candidate does not pass, they can retake the test up to three times in a two-year period. Exam scores can be sent to a third party by ordering a score verification request.

Recent/Future Developments

The National Counselor Exam is changed for each administration. Questions are drawn from a pool. All questions undergo review and validity testing. Out of the 200 questions, only 160 are scored and the remaining 40 are used for statistics for future exams. Even though exam questions are changed, the format remains the same.

Human Growth and Development

This section covers the works and teachings of fundamental thinkers in the field of human growth and development. Important terms are provided in a glossary at the end of this section.

Categories of Human Development

Human development is dynamic, with a number of components that influence and interact with one another. There are three main components of human development:

- Physical: Physical human development includes factors such as biological and physiological growth, emergence/refinement of gross and fine motor skills, speaking, and coordination of larger physical systems, such as hand-eye coordination.

- Cognitive: Cognitive human development includes factors such as noticing and utilizing the senses, memory, the ability to imagine, understanding abstract concepts, understanding/using language, and processing one's perceptions and emotions.

- Psychosocial: Psychosocial human development includes factors such as cultivating and nurturing personal relationships and contributing to and existing in one's society. How an individual responds to his or her environment is also a factor.

Erikson's Stages of Development

German-born American psychologist Erik Erikson (1902–1994) first suggested that children's development is shaped not only by their genetics, but also by society. This idea became known as the theory of psychosocial development. Erikson is best known for the importance he placed on the constructs of conflict negotiation and identity crisis in the development of human personality. He hypothesized that humans develop by progressing through a series of eight psychological crises (stages) that focus on these two constructs. An individual's reactions to these two constructs shift both personally and interpersonally, as he or she grows older and experiences more events. Successful navigation of each crisis helps to build virtues that assist in handling future problems.

Eight Stages, Virtues, and Ages
- Trust vs. mistrust: develops hope and occurs during infancy
- Autonomy vs. shame: develops will and occurs in ages one-and-a-half to three
- Initiative vs. guilt: develops purpose and occurs from ages two to six
- Industry vs. inferiority: develops competence and occurs from ages six to twelve
- Identity vs. diffusion: develops fidelity and occurs from ages twelve to eighteen
- Intimacy vs. isolation: develops love and occurs from ages nineteen to forty
- Generativity vs. self-absorption: develops care and occurs from ages forty to sixty-five
- Integrity vs. despair: develops wisdom and takes place from age sixty-five to death

Erikson believed that experiencing obstacles within any of these eight stages led to psychopathology, but that positive experiences later in life could provide healing for earlier negative experiences. To this end, these factors shaped an individual's personality over the course of his or her lifespan.

Psychoanalytic and Psychosexual Development Theory

Austrian neurologist Sigmund Freud (1856–1939) developed psychoanalytic theory as a means of examining the process of personality development, in order to treat psychopathologies clinically. It focused on examining the client's subconscious and unconscious thoughts and desires, as well as the internal struggles between biological urges and social expectations.

Psychoanalysis dominated psychological treatment options in the United States from the early 1900s through the 1970s, and Freud's work influenced psychosocial theories later developed by other pioneers such as Erik Erikson. Influential texts written during this time included Freud's *The Interpretation of Dreams* (1900), *Beyond the Pleasure Principle* (1920), and *The Ego and the Id* (1923).

Freud believed that personality development took place primarily during childhood and involved the dynamics of three components within the human conscious: the id, the ego, and the superego.

Freud believed personality development was greatly influenced through five stages of psychosexual development: oral, anal, phallic, latency, and genital. Each of these stages exists to resolve conflict between the id, which is driven to satisfy physical urge, and the superego, which is driven to act in a socially acceptable manner. The resolution between the two ultimately develops the ego, which is the basis for the individual's personality, what Freud referred to as the self. According to Freudian thought, an inability to find a resolution between the id and the superego can lead to psychopathology.

Piaget's Theory of Development

Swiss psychologist Jean Piaget (1896–1980) produced a theory of development that categorized stages by age and intellectual ability. Piaget believed that although the actual age when one reaches a stage may vary slightly, the sequential order always stays the same. These stages indicate the level of skill and understanding with which one can perceive the world, and they become more detailed and complex with each progression.

Piaget's four stages of development are as follows:

- Sensorimotor stage: (Birth to roughly two years of age) In the sensorimotor stage, infants learn to interact with their environment, using their senses to roll, crawl, walk, and make sounds as a precursor to language. One of the most important accomplishments in this stage is known as *object permanence*. This is when a child realizes that an object or person still exists even though the child may not see them.

- Preoperational stage: (Roughly age two to seven) In the preoperational stage, toddlers and small children increase their language skills and develop imagination and a sense of relational time.

- Concrete operational stage: (Age seven to twelve) In the concrete operational stage, older children learn to reason and to think of others.

- Formal operational stage: (Age twelve and beyond) The formal operational stage lasts the rest of the individual's lifetime as he or she learns to think critically, develop and test hypotheses, and build deeper relationships.

Kohlberg's Theory

Lawrence Kohlberg (1927–1987), an American psychologist, is known for his work examining how people develop morals. His theory of moral development stated that individuals progressed sequentially through three levels, each with two stages. Moral development tends to begin in the preschool to young childhood age range.

Preconventional Morality

The first level, preconventional morality, is when individuals are influenced by reward and punishment.

- Stage 1: Orientation to obedience and punishment. Children act as prescribed by a figure of authority.
- Stage 2: Individualism and exchange. Children begin to understand that there are gray areas to right and wrong.

Conventional Morality

The second level, conventional morality, occurs when individuals behave morally to win external approval by peers or society and to cultivate positive relationships.

- Stage 3: Good relationships. Individuals seek to gain approval from others.
- Stage 4: Maintaining social order. Moral behavior is determined by social and cultural law, legal obligations, and one's sense of duty.

Postconventional Morality

The third level, postconventional morality, occurs when individuals engage in abstract thinking and development of personal moral principles.

- Stage 5: Social contract and individual rights. Individuals act in a way that considers society and its welfare, rather than maintaining a singular motivation of self-interest as the basis for moral behavior.
- Stage 6: Universal principles. Moral thinking is influenced by respecting universal justice for all people.

Kohlberg believed that one could not progress to a stage without mastering the one before it and that many never reach stages five or six.

Oedipus and Electra Complexes

The Oedipus and Electra complexes are a component of the phallic stage of psychosexual stages of development, occurring between three and five years of age. Freud believed that, in this stage, individuals become aware of differences in anatomy and social characteristics between the two genders.

Young males experience the Oedipus complex, where the boy wants to remove the presence of his father to possess his mother. The young boy fears that if his father discovers this motivation, it will result in castration. Young girls experience the Electra complex, where they want to remove the presence of the mother in order to possess the father. Freud believed these complexes resolved themselves when the young child took on the characteristics of the same-sex parent and therefore further developed aspects of their identity.

Bowlby and Harlow's Theories on Attachment and Bonding

British psychologist, psychoanalyst, and psychiatrist John Bowlby (1907–1990) first used the term *attachment*. His work with the attachment theory resulted in the belief that for a child to develop healthily, he or she must be able to have a strong attachment—a loving, nurturing relationship—with at least one main caretaker, typically one of the parents.

The ability to form a strong attachment at this age provided security, stability, and self-esteem for the individual later in life. It also promoted independence and the desire to seek out new learning opportunities, which, in turn, provided better opportunities for individual development. Those with weaker attachments in infancy and young childhood might be more anxious and tentative, as well as less willing to engage in new experiences.

Bowlby was a doctoral student of American psychologist Harry Harlow (1905–1981), who worked with monkeys to understand and explain human behavior and development related to mother-baby interaction and social isolation. Through his experiments, he suggested that infants have an innate need to be held close, kept warm, shown affection, and nourished—not only with food, water, and shelter, but also through love and physical closeness. Harlow observed that infant monkeys who did not receive these things showed signs of social impairment, aloofness, aggression, and other atypical behaviors. These monkeys also failed to show nurturing behaviors to any offspring produced. He believed these findings held true in humans.

Imprinting and Konrad Lorenz

Austrian zoologist, ornithologist, and ethologist Konrad Lorenz (1903–1989) hatched ducklings and goslings in an incubator to show how the newly hatched birds would imprint on any entity they saw in the hours after hatching. This entity could have been their mother, Lorenz, or a number of inanimate objects. The ducklings or goslings would begin to follow the entity and take on its characteristics. Lorenz defined this period as the critical period for imprinting. This discovery supported the idea that some learned behaviors must take place at pre-determined stages of development.

Major Theme in Levinson's *The Seasons of a Man's Life*

American psychologist Daniel Levinson (1920–1994) focused his studies on adult subjects to create his Stage-Crisis View, in which there are stable periods and transitional periods in life, and suggested stages of development throughout the lifespan:

- Early adult transition: age seventeen to twenty-two
- Entering the adult world: age twenty-two to twenty-eight
- Age thirty transition: age twenty-eight to thirty-three
- Settling down: age thirty-three to forty
- Mid-life transition: age forty to forty-five
- Entering middle adulthood: age forty-five to fifty
- Late adulthood transition: age sixty to sixty-five
- Late adulthood: age sixty-five to eighty

These stages present social conflicts that must be resolved. Levinson also proposed that a midlife crisis is part of a normal, healthy development. The Stage-Crisis View theory was the premise of his renowned

text, *The Seasons of a Man's Life*, which examines the feelings, dreams, and behaviors of men throughout their lifespans and how these influence the way a man structures his life.

Maslow's Hierarchy of Needs, Gesell's Maturationist Theory, and the Behaviorism Learning Approach

American psychologist Abraham Maslow (1908–1970) developed the Hierarchy of Needs model—which states that all humans have inherent needs—in order to explain the motives for human behavior. Basic biological needs must be met before an individual is motivated to engage in behaviors that will fulfill deeper psychological needs. Maslow's Hierarchy of Needs consists of five levels, presented in a pyramid shape.

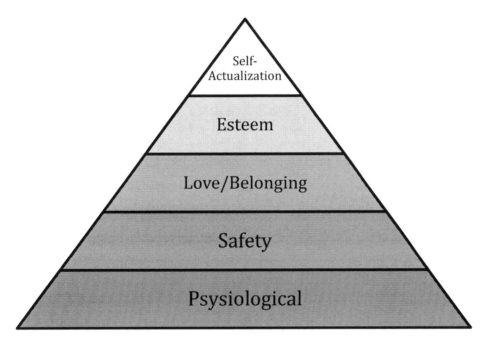

1. The bottom, foundational category covers *physiological needs*—e.g., food, water, and shelter.

2. In ascending order, the next category is *safety needs*—e.g., a safe living environment and stable financial means.

3. *Love and belonging needs* is the next category—e.g., healthy relationships with other people and fitting into one's culture and society.

4. *Esteem needs* is the category next to the top—e.g., intrinsic self-respect and self-esteem.

5. The top of the pyramid holds the category of *self-actualization needs*—e.g., discovering one's purpose in life and fulfilling one's potential.

The interpretation of Maslow's Hierarchy of Needs and what satisfies each level often varies globally by culture, physical geography, and socioeconomic status.

American pediatrician and psychologist Arnold Gesell (1880–1961) conducted longitudinal observational studies over fifty years to produce a number of theories regarding human development. His maturationist theory states that beginning at the fetal stage, individuals will follow set, linear steps of physical and cognitive development. Gesell argued that human development is primarily governed by an individual's genetic makeup. External influences (e.g., society, parents, siblings, and teachers) are most effective when their actions support the physiological progress that will take place.

Behaviorism is a broad term that describes the scientific approach one might take to understand human and animal behavior. Some common themes in this practice include the assumption that individual history, internal motivation, and external influences—such as reward or punishment in response to particular actions—play a large role in predicting behavior. Influential theorists include Ivan Pavlov, B.F Skinner, John Watson, and Edward Thorndike.

Work of Anna Freud Jean Baker Miller, Carol Tavris, Nancy Chodorow, Harriet Lerner, Carol Gilligan, and Gail Sheehy

A number of American female psychologists, psychiatrists, and psychoanalysts have been influential in shaping psychological research that pertains to development in women and in serving as leaders in feminist theory:

Anna Freud (1895–1982) made significant contributions to the field of psychoanalysis, especially regarding the ego and child development. She was the youngest daughter of Sigmund Freud. Some of her works include *Introduction to Psychoanalysis: Lectures for Child Analysts and Teachers* and *Ego and the Mechanisms of Defense*.

Jean Baker Miller (1927–2006) is best known for authoring the revered text *Toward a New Psychology of Women* (1976). She is also known for her work with Relational-Cultural Theory, which focuses on how culture affects relationships and how healthy connections with others are an integral part of psychological health and personal growth. These ideas often played a role in diagnosing and treating depression in women.

Carol Tavris (1944–) promoted critical thinking and evidence-based research in psychology, focusing on cognitive dissonance, and her views that many female psychological "issues" are actually social beliefs that are not backed by science.

Nancy Chodorow (1944–) authored the renowned text *Psychoanalysis and the Sociology of Gender* (1978). Her research focused on mothering, gender systems, how the family influences female roles in society, and gender identity formation.

Harriet Lerner (1944–) is best known for her work regarding gender roles in marriage, cultural gender norms, and how women can balance self-care with other competing priorities in their lives.

Carol Gilligan (1936–) was a research assistant to Lawrence Kohlberg and openly argued that his theories of moral development were male-focused and did not apply to females. Her research focused on the development of morals and ethics in women, and she authored *In a Different Voice* in 1982.

Gail Sheehy (1937–) is an author and journalist by trade and wrote a book entitled *Passages* (1976) that supports many of the beliefs and ideas of feminist psychologists. This book covers the different periods of life that women progress through and the emotions that occur in each one. The Library of Congress honored *Passages* as one of the top ten most influential books of its time.

Scheme Developed by William Perry

William Perry (1913–1998) examined the development of college students during his professorship at the Harvard Graduate School of Education. He developed a scheme that focused on learning and the retention of information, the act and experience of knowing something, and how mental functions, like thinking and reasoning, develop in relation to knowledge. In this scheme, Perry lists four categories of development that college students will progress sequentially through most, and sometimes all, of these categories:

- Dualism: Students view knowledge in binary categories—right answers versus wrong answers. They believe teachers hold the "right" answers, and the student's job is to learn and retain these answers.

- Multiplicity: Students begin to realize that gray areas can be found in knowledge and that people may have differences of opinion in unproven matters.

- Relativism: Students begin to examine opinions systematically, to validate or debunk them in various contexts of knowledge.

- Commitment in relativism: Students choose to commit to certain beliefs based on personal opinions, beliefs, interests, needs, and goals. Typically, they realize that they should remain flexible in their commitments, since new information can be presented at any time that could impact their beliefs.

Intelligence vs. Emotional Intelligence

Intelligence describes the ability of an individual to learn and retain information, to think critically about information, and to apply that information to theoretical or real-world problems. It typically focuses on an individual's ability to absorb and work with abstract concepts and concrete information. The Intelligence Quotient (IQ) index describes an individual's intellectual ability.

The concept of emotional intelligence, measured by the Emotional Quotient (EQ) index, takes into account how an individual perceives feelings, the nonverbal and verbal communication of others, and other fluid concepts. This includes understanding group dynamics, interpersonal relationships, social norms, and self-awareness. It typically focuses on an individual's ability to understand personal motivations and feelings, and on his or her ability to interact positively with surrounding people and environment.

Here are the five components of emotional intelligence:

Five Components of Emotional Intelligence

	Definition	Characteristics
Self-Awareness	Identifying one's own emotions, motivations, and desires, and the effects they have on others	Confidence Sense of Humor Awareness of Others' Perception of Self
Self-Regulation	Being able to express oneself appropriately by controlling one's own emotions before acting	Honesty Adaptability Disarming in Tense Situations
Motivation	Exhibiting self-motivation or the desire to better one's self; eagerness to learn	Initiative Determination
Empathy	Being able to understand others' emotions as if they were one's own	Intuition of Others' Reactions Awareness of Others' Needs
Social Skill	Being able to manage relationships and construct social networks	Leadership Communication Managing Conflict

Spirituality Influences on Personality Development

Spirituality is a broad term that encompasses seeking the meaning of one's life, a connection to a higher power, and/or a connection to an unknown force beyond one's physical being. Beliefs that people hold about spirituality often influence how their morals, ethics, altruism, and motivations develop. Though a spiritual individual does not have to follow an organized religion, some religions directly state that human development occurs as a part of practicing the religion.

Id, Ego, and Superego

From the Freudian school of thought, the id, ego, and superego are believed to be the three main components that make up one's psyche. Freud believed the interaction of these three components gave rise to one's personality. According to Freud's pleasure principle, people are naturally drawn to engage in behaviors that provide direct, immediate sensations of pleasure. This motive is governed by the id, which seeks to fulfill one's most basic needs. Freud believed people are born with only the id, which helps newborns communicate and fulfill their most basic needs, such as being fed or comforted.

Over time, as the individual has more experiences with his or her environment, parents, caretakers, teachers, and society in general, morals and rules are learned. Noticing and implementing these rules

shapes the morals of the person, which is governed by the superego—sometimes referred to as one's conscience. The superego is relatively restrained and can be described as the opposite end of the spectrum from the demanding urges of the id.

The third component of the psyche, the ego, develops to balance the superego and the id. Freud believed that in an individual with a healthy psyche, the ego is the strongest of the three components. This allows the individual to balance satisfying his or her personal urges with what is most appropriate for society, as well as taking into consideration the thoughts and feelings of other people.

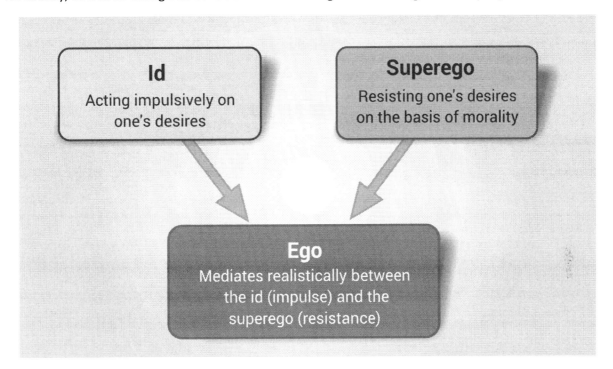

Various Theorists

Many developmental theorists have been covered in this section, but there are some additional key thinkers to consider:

- Alfred Adler (1870–1937): Austrian medical doctor and psychotherapist, known for establishing the school of individual psychology and for work on the inferiority complex and how it shapes personality

- Mary Ainsworth (1931–1999): American-Canadian psychologist, known for work regarding emotional attachment in infants and the Strange Situation experiment

- Albert Bandura (1925–): American psychologist who theorized that learning takes place socially through observation and imitation of others and that not all behaviors are conditioned

- Jerome Bruner (1915–2016): American psychologist who focused on how children learn, was instrumental in starting the national Head Start program, and believed that any individual could learn a topic if it is organized and presented appropriately

- Ivan Pavlov (1849–1936): Russian physiologist who developed the theory of classical conditioning, best known for experimenting with dogs (the Pavlovian Experiment), where he

rang a bell at the exact same instant a dog saw food, causing the dog to salivate and, over repeated instances, to salivate at the sound of the bell alone

- B.F. Skinner (1904–1990): American psychologist who developed the theory of behaviorism and the term *operant conditioning*

- John B. Watson (1878–1958): American psychologist who introduced the school of thought behind behaviorism and conducted the well-known Little Albert experiment

- Viktor Frankl (1905–1997): Austrian neurologist, psychologist, and Holocaust survivor, known for developing logotherapy, a type of existentialist theory, and writing *Man's Search for Meaning* (1946). Termed the phrase *paradoxical intention*.

- Eric Berne (1910–1970): Canadian psychiatrist who studied game theory, developed transactional analysis, and wrote the best-selling book *Games People Play* (1964), which explained social interactions

- Edward Thorndike (1874–1979): American behavioral psychologist who developed the operant conditioning theory that influenced Skinner, famous for experiments with cats learning puzzle boxes

Important Terms

Assertiveness Training: a form of behavior therapy that helps people empower themselves, encouraging them to find a balance between passivity and aggression

Behaviorism: the study of quantifiable and observable human or animal behavior

Castration Anxiety: part of Freudian theory, a young boy's fear during the phallic psychosexual stage that his father will remove his penis

Classical Conditioning: based on studies of Pavlov, behavior that is learned by creating an association between two stimuli, resulting in a response to previously neutral stimulus to elicit the conditioned response

Cognitive Dissonance: when a person's beliefs, thoughts, and attitudes are inconsistent, or when their beliefs contradict their actions. Cognitive dissonance can create an uncomfortable feeling in a person, causing self-doubt and hesitation.

Conditioned Response: a learned response that is developed through conditioning, such as Pavlov's dogs salivating at the sound of a bell

Ego: in Freudian theory, the part of the human psyche that tries to balance the primal desires of the id with the moral extremes of the superego

Fixation: in Freudian theory, an instance where a child becomes unable to progress from one psychosexual stage to the next

Id: in Freudian theory, the part of the human psyche that focuses on physical needs and gratification

Identification: in Freudian theory, when a young child copies gender-specific behaviors of the same-sex parent to progress past an Oedipus/Electra complex

Imprinting: a behavioral event that occurs in the initial few hours after birth where the infant bonds to a specific entity and imitates its behaviors, easily seen in ducklings and goslings, but theoretically believed to apply to humans

Interval Reinforcement Schedules: target behavior that is reinforced after a certain period of time. The two types of interval reinforcement are fixed interval and variable interval. Fixed interval reinforcement determines a specific interval of time. Variable interval reinforcement occurs after an average length of time.

Little Albert Experiment: experiment by John Watson that demonstrated how the principles of behaviorism could be used to condition a child to fear a white rat, which was then generalized to other white, furry objects

Negative Reinforcement: learned behavior meant to avoid a negative stimulus

Object Permanence: a construct of the Piaget stages of development that occurs when infants realize that objects continue to exist even if those objects are taken out of view, usually between seven to nine months of age

Operant Conditioning: according to Skinner, learning that occurs as a result of direct consequences to the behavior, such as rewards or punishment

Paradoxical Intention: developed by Viktor Frankl, this term suggests deliberately engaging in a neurotic habit or thought for the sole purpose of identifying and eradicating it

Penis Envy: in Freudian theory, during the phallic psychosexual stage, a young girl's desire to have a penis in order to have more in common with her father

Pleasure Principle: in Freudian theory, the innate desire to engage in behavior that will bring pleasurable sensations and avoid pain

Positive Reinforcement: rewarding a particular behavior to make that behavior more likely in the future

Ratio Reinforcement Schedules: target behavior is reinforced after a certain number of occurrences. The two schedules of reinforcement are fixed ratio and variable ratio. Fixed ratio is reinforcing a behavior after a specific number of occurrences. Variable ratio is reinforcing a behavior after an approximate number of occurrences.

Strange Situation Experiment: first conducted by Ainsworth, infants aged nine to eighteen months placed in a foreign room with their caregivers and a stranger to observe the infants' attachment styles

Superego: Freudian concept regarding the part of the human psyche that serves as one's conscience and encourages the individual to act in socially and morally acceptable ways

Transference: the act of a client projecting feelings towards another person, typically an authority figure from childhood, onto the counselor

Unconditioned Response: the natural reaction to a stimulus, such as dogs salivating at the sight of food

Practice Questions

1. Mary is playing with her eight-month-old baby brother, Joe. Mary shakes a rattle in front of Joe and then hides it under a blanket. Joe crawls over to the blanket and reaches under it to pull out the rattle. Which cognitive milestone has Joe developed?
   a. Self-awareness
   b. Perception of social cues
   c. Object permanence
   d. Bonding

2. *The Ego and the Id* (1923) is an influential text in the field of psychology written by whom?
   a. Erik Erikson
   b. Sigmund Freud
   c. Mary Ainsworth
   d. John B. Watson

3. Jean Piaget's formal operational stage corresponds with the approximate ages of _____ and focuses on the development of skills like _____.
   a. Two years to seven years; language development and imagination
   b. Birth to two years; crawling, walking, and making sounds
   c. Twelve years and beyond; critical thinking, developing and testing hypotheses, and building deep relationships
   d. Seven years to ten years; reasoning and empathy

4. Which of the following is an index that measures someone's cognitive, critical, and abstract thinking abilities?
   a. Intelligence
   b. Intellectual Achievement
   c. Intelligence Quotient
   d. Emotional Quotient

5. Lawrence Kohlberg's theory of developing moral principles consists of preconventional, conventional, and postconventional morality. Each of these levels contains two stages. Kohlberg believed people rarely achieved which of the following stages in his theory of moral development?
   a. Stages one and two
   b. Stages one and three
   c. Stages four and five
   d. Stages five and six

6. Who was a student and researcher of Lawrence Kohlberg and believed Kohlberg's moral development theories did not apply to women?
   a. Carol Gilligan
   b. Nancy Chodorow
   c. Anna Freud
   d. Jean Piaget

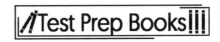

7. Six-year-old Natalie lives near a small pond. Natalie happens to be around the pond shortly after a duck's eggs hatch. One of the ducklings sees Natalie and begins following her around incessantly and trying to copy her mannerisms. She walks home, but the duckling does not leave her alone. This is an example of what?
    a. Cognitive development
    b. Motor skills
    c. Imprinting
    d. Postpartum filtering

8. Jean Piaget's preoperational stage corresponds with the approximate ages of _____ and focuses on the development of skills like _____.
    a. Birth to two years; rolling, crawling, walking, and making sounds
    b. Seven years to twelve years; reasoning and empathy
    c. Twelve years to thirty years; building deep relationships and getting a job
    d. Two years to seven years; language development and imagination

9. Which of the following is an index that measures someone's ability to connect with others, develop relationships, and show empathy?
    a. Intelligence Quotient
    b. Emotional Quotient
    c. Emotional Achievement
    d. Emotional Handling

10. Jack is training his Labrador puppy to fetch. Every time the puppy retrieves a thrown object and places it in Jack's hand, Jack gives the puppy a bacon treat. This is an example of what?
    a. Positive reinforcement
    b. Modeling
    c. Extinguishing
    d. Negative reinforcement

11. Three-year-old Sara used to be very fond of her mother, but now always seems grumpy around her. Instead, Sara prefers to spend time with her father and gets very excited to see him. Meanwhile, any time her mother tries to show affection, Sara gets upset and pushes her mother away. Her mother feels sad about this, but Sigmund Freud would say that Sara is working through which of the following?
    a. An id moment
    b. The Electra complex
    c. The Oedipus complex
    d. Latency stage

12. Jean Piaget's concrete operational stage corresponds with the approximate ages of _____ and focuses on the development of skills like _____.
    a. Twelve years and beyond; building relationships and learning to think critically
    b. Birth to two years; language development and imagination
    c. Two years to seven years; language development and imagination
    d. Seven years to twelve years; reasoning and empathy

13. Nancy Chodorow, Harriet Lerner, Carol Tavris, and Jean Baker Miller are all leading researchers who have focused on what?
    a. Psychoanalytic counseling
    b. Classical conditioning
    c. Feminist psychology
    d. The psychology of the industrial age

14. Five-year-old Ben has started to hit and kick his dad, especially if he shows any affection toward Ben's mother. At night, Ben screams to sleep in his parent's bed and tries to create a physical barrier between his mother and father. He is always in a much better mood if his father is not physically present. One day, Ben suddenly begins to act very shy around his father, while copying most of his mannerisms. Freud would say Ben is illustrating which of the following?
    a. Anal stage
    b. Penis envy
    c. The Oedipus complex
    d. The Electra complex

15. Arnold Gesell is one of the few leaders in psychological thought who believed that the progression of one's development is primarily _____.
    a. Sequential through various socially influenced stages
    b. Genetic and hereditary
    c. A direct function of parenting
    d. Related to direct cultural ties

16. The eight chronological sequences of development listed below mark a theory established by whom?

Infancy, Toddler, Preschooler, School Age, Adolescence,
Young Adulthood, Middle Adulthood, Late Adulthood

    a. Jean Piaget
    b. Gail Sheehy
    c. Erik Erikson
    d. Abraham Maslow

17. Joe's parents divorced when he was six years old, and his father moved out of the house. He is now receiving therapy and has become very angry with his male therapist, fearing the therapist will abandon him. Joe's reaction is an example of what?
    a. Remorse
    b. Fixation
    c. Negative reinforcement
    d. Transference

18. Jean Piaget's sensorimotor stage corresponds with the approximate ages of _____ and focuses on the development of skills like _____.
    a. Birth to two years; rolling, crawling, walking, and making sounds
    b. Two to seven years; language development and imagination
    c. Seven years to twelve years; learning to reason and think of others
    d. Twelve years through adulthood; building deep relationships and learning to think critically

22

19. William Perry focused a theory of development on the cognitive abilities, conceptions of knowing, and knowledge application practices of which of the following?
    a. Geese
    b. Monkeys
    c. College students
    d. New parents

20. The four progressive stages of William Perry's scheme, which focused on the learning, information retention, and knowledge application of college students, fall in which order?
    a. Dualism, multiplicity, relativism, commitment to relativism
    b. Dualism, relativism, multiplicity, omnipotence
    c. Relativism, dualism, commitment to relativism, multiplicity
    d. Relativism, commitment to relativism, dualism, multiplicity

21. An individual leaves early for their commute to work to avoid traffic. This is an example of what?
    a. Modeling
    b. Negative reinforcement
    c. Positive reinforcement
    d. Classical conditioning

22. What are the three domains of study in human development?
    a. Physical, cognitive, and social
    b. Physical, cognitive, and psychosocial
    c. Neurological, physiological, and pathologies
    d. Environmental, internal, and spiritual

23. Who authored *The Seasons of a Man's Life*, which examines the feelings, dreams, and behaviors of men throughout their lifespans?
    a. Carol Tavris
    b. Daniel Levinson
    c. Lawrence Kohlberg
    d. Alfred Adler

24. Of the id, the ego, and the superego, what is the strongest component of the individual's psyche in a healthy individual?
    a. The id
    b. The ego
    c. The superego
    d. A healthy individual will have all of the above components existing in equal balance, where one part is not stronger than another.

25. Who wrote *Passages*, a book honored by the Library of Congress as one of the top ten influential books of its time?
    a. John B. Watson
    b. Mary Ainsworth
    c. Gail Sheehy
    d. Daniel Levinson

26. Harry Harlow noticed that monkeys who did not receive consistent warmth or affection from a maternal figure were more likely to be which of the following?

a. Less warm or affectionate to their own offspring
b. Aloof and/or angry
c. Socially impaired
d. All of the above

Answer Explanations

1. C: Joe has developed the cognitive milestone of object permanence. Joe realizes that the rattle still exists even though he cannot see it, a cognitive skill that develops between seven to nine months of age. Choice *A* is incorrect; self-awareness is one of the components of emotional intelligence, and Joe has not demonstrated these characteristics, which include confidence and sense of humor. Choice *B* is incorrect; although children pick up social cues from a very young age, there is no indication of Joe mimicking Mary's body language or responding to her socially. Choice *D* is tempting; Mary is, in a way, bonding with Joe by playing with him. However, it is not the best answer choice. The question asks for a cognitive milestone, and bonding is not considered a cognitive milestone, although it is important for healthy emotional maturity.

2. B: Sigmund Freud wrote *The Ego and the Id*, which is famous for its exploration of the human psyche concerning the ego, the id, and the super-ego. Choice *A* is incorrect; Erik Erikson was a psychologist who suggested that children's development is shaped by society as well as genetics, and wrote *Childhood and Society* and *Identity: Youth and Crisis*. Choice *C* is incorrect; Mary Ainsworth was a psychologist who is known for researching emotional attachment in infants. Finally, John B. Watson introduced behaviorism and is known for conducting the Little Albert experiment.

3. C: Twelve years and beyond; critical thinking, developing and testing hypotheses, and building deep relationships. According to Piaget, the formal operational stage is the final stage people experience and lasts from age twelve through all of the years of adulthood. It is a stage that brings constant learning and consists of achieving skills like critical thinking, continuous experimenting to understand life, and building strong, long-lasting relationships.

4. C: Intelligence Quotient. More commonly known as IQ, this index measures someone's intellectual ability. The average person's IQ falls between 90 and 110. Over 125 is considered exceptional, and under seventy is considered intellectually deficient. Choices *A* and *B* are too broad to be considered actual terms in psychology. Choice *D* is an index used to measure someone's ability to show empathy and connect with others, so this is incorrect.

5. D: Five and six. Stages five and six of this theory consist of acting in a way that considers society, the welfare of others, and respecting universal justice for all people. These two stages differ from the first four stages, which focus primarily on the self and self-development. Stage 1 is orientation to obedience and punishment, and stage 2 is individualism and exchange. Most people make it to these stages, so Choices *A* and *B* are incorrect. Stage 3 is seeking good relationships, and stage 4 is maintaining social order, so Choice *C* is incorrect.

6. A: Carol Gilligan was a student and researcher of Lawrence Kohlberg. Gilligan argued that women underwent completely different personal and social experiences from men to shape their moral standings and that Kohlberg only considered men's experiences when he developed his theories. Choice *B* is incorrect; Nancy Chodorow focused on mothering, gender systems, female roles in society, and gender identity formation, and wrote the text *Psychoanalysis and the Sociology of Gender*. Choice *C* is incorrect; Anna Freud made contributions to psychoanalysis regarding the ego and child development. Choice *D* is incorrect; Jean Piaget was a psychologist who is known for the four stages of development.

7. C: This is an example of imprinting. Many animals take on the characteristics of the first object they visibly see and begin to take on its mannerisms as a way of learning how to interact with their environment. Typically, newborns imprint on their mother, but some can even imprint on inanimate objects. Choice *A*, cognitive development, is a field of psychological study focusing on a child's mental development, and does not make sense in this context. Choice *B*, motor skills, is the ability to perform muscle-and-nerve acts producing movement, so this is also incorrect. Choice *D*, postpartum filtering, is a made-up phrase and does not exist in the terminology of psychology.

8. D: Two years to seven years; language development and imagination. According to Piaget's developmental theory, the preoperational stage is the second developmental stage people experience, and it consists of achieving deeper cognitive functions, such as understanding language and the concept of make-believe.

9. B: Emotional Quotient. Also known as EQ, this index is lesser known than its IQ counterpart. People with high EQ tend to have better interpersonal and leadership achievements. Choice *A* is an index that measures someone's cognitive and critical thinking abilities, so this choice is incorrect. Choices *C* and *D* are too broad and do not refer to a measurement of emotional intelligence.

10. A: This is an example of positive reinforcement. This is a type of behavior teaching technique that involves rewarding a desired behavior when that behavior is shown. It ultimately teaches the person or animal who is showing the behavior that the behavior is associated with adding (thus, positive) a pleasurable experience. Choice *B*, modeling, is a technique used by counselors by "modeling" a certain behavior so that clients may behave in a similar fashion, so this is incorrect in this context. Choice *C*, extinguishing, is the process of ending maladaptive thought pattern or behavior, so this is also incorrect. Choice *D*, negative reinforcement, refers to changing a behavior by removing an unwanted consequence, so this is also incorrect.

11. B: Sara is working through the Electra complex. According to Freud, girls will exhibit antagonistic behavior toward their mothers and become very possessive of their fathers at some point during the ages of three and five. Choice *A* is incorrect; there is no such thing as an "id" moment. The "id" is the most primitive part of the mind based on the pleasure principle. Choice *C* is incorrect; the Oedipus complex is when boys exhibit antagonist behavior toward their fathers. Choice *D* is incorrect; the latency stage is one of Freud's five stages of psychosexual development, wherein children will redirect their focus from the opposite sex parent to developing the self.

12. D: Seven years to twelve years; reasoning and empathy. According to Piaget, the concrete operational stage is the third developmental stage people experience, and it consists of achieving skills like reasoning and understanding the feelings of other people.

13. C: Feminist psychology. These women, along with others, paved the way for deconstructing previously widely accepted psychological thought to support women's mental and physical health issues, social issues, and gender inequality issues.

14. C: Ben is illustrating the Oedipus complex. According to Freud, boys will exhibit antagonist behavior toward their fathers and become very possessive of their mothers at some point during the ages of three and five. Additionally, boys will try to identify with his father's characteristics to ultimately progress through this complex. Choice A is incorrect; the anal stage is one of Freud's five psychosexual stages; the anal stage typically involves toilet training. Choice B is incorrect; penis envy refers to the supposed female envy of the male's possession of a penis. Choice D is incorrect; the Electra Complex refers to when girls exhibit antagonistic behavior toward their mothers and become possessive of their fathers.

15. B: Genetic and hereditary. Gesell believed that developmental progress was mainly cognitive, was based on genetic and hereditary factors, and would take place regardless of social influences. He believed that social influences could help development only if they were tailored to the stage that was already occurring.

16. C: This theory was established by Erik Erikson. These eight stages represent distinct psychosocial periods where an individual learns how to manage specific conflicts and identity crises. Choice A, Jean Piaget, developed a theory of development with four stages: sensorimotor stage, preoperational stage, concrete operational stage, and formal operational stage. Choice B, Gail Sheehy, was a feminist psychologist who wrote *Passages*. Choice D, Abraham Maslow, developed Maslow's Hierarchy of Needs, which states that basic biological needs must be met in order for an individual to engage in behaviors that satisfy deeper psychological needs.

17. D: Joe's reaction is an example of transference. Joe is transferring feelings toward his father onto his therapist, which may be beneficial in resolving his childhood issues. Choice A is incorrect; remorse is a feeling of deep regret or of a wrong committed, and does not make sense in this context. Choice B is incorrect; in Freudian theory, fixation occurs when a child is unable to progress from one psychosexual stage to the next. Choice C is incorrect; negative reinforcement is a learned behavior meant to avoid negative stimulus.

18. A: Birth to two years; rolling, crawling, walking, and making sounds. According to Piaget's developmental theory, the sensorimotor stage is the first developmental stage people experience, and it consists of achieving basic sensory and motor skills. Choice B is incorrect; language development and imagination are skills in the preoperational stage, roughly age two to seven. Choice C is incorrect; learning to reason and think of others is known as the concrete operational stage and happens during ages seven to twelve years. Choice D is incorrect; this is the formal operational stage (twelve years and beyond), which also includes developing and testing hypotheses, in addition to building relationships and learning to think critically.

19. C: College students. Perry, a professor at Harvard's Graduate School of Education, was interested in knowing how college students learned and retained information over the course of their college careers.

20. A: Dualism, multiplicity, relativism, commitment to relativism. These are the four progressive stages, in order, that Perry believed college students progressed through in college. The stages involve believing that all questions have binary answers, then realizing that some knowledge is unknown and unproven, then forming opinions about answers to questions, and finally, committing to one's beliefs.

21. B: This is an example of negative reinforcement. This type of behavioral technique involves changing a behavior by removing its unwanted consequence. It intends to teach that the behavior (leaving late for work) is associated with an unfavorable experience (being stuck in traffic). The negative aspect is the act of removing, as opposed to positive reinforcement that adds a consequence, such as a reward for a desired behavior, which makes Choice *C* incorrect. Choice *A*, modeling, is when a counselor models a behavior for a client so they can behave in a similar fashion. Choice *D*, classical conditioning, is when two stimuli are paired repeatedly, and the response over the first stimulus will eventually also become a response to the second stimulus by itself. This is shown in Pavlov's dog, where eventually the dog salivates to the sound of a bell, even if there is no food paired with it anymore.

22. B: Physical, cognitive, and psychosocial. Physical studies include topics like biological and physiological growth and coordination of larger physical systems. Cognitive studies include topics that take place in the brain, such as reasoning, memory, and perception. Psychosocial studies include cultivating and nurturing personal relationships, or how an individual responds to his or her environment.

23. B: Daniel Levinson authored *The Seasons of a Man's Life*. This book is considered one of Levinson's most pivotal works, and examines how men's feelings influence the way they structure their lives. Choice *A*, Carol Tavris, was a feminist psychologist who promoted critical thinking and evidence-based research to show that many female psychological "issues" were social beliefs and not backed by science. Choice *C*, Lawrence Kohlberg, is known for his theory of moral development. Choice *D*, Alfred Adler, developed the concept of birth order that showed how order of birth played a major role in an individual's personality.

24. B: The strongest component of an individual's psyche in a healthy individual is the ego. Freud believed that in a healthy individual, the ego is the strongest component, and thus, it is able to mitigate the basic needs of the id with the overly moralistic discipline of the superego, making Choices *A*, *C*, and *D* incorrect.

25. C: Gail Sheehy wrote *Passages*. This book chronicles the stages of emotion and different obstacles that women face throughout life, as influenced by the stage of development and social status. Choice *A*, John B. Watson, was an American psychologist who introduced the school of thought behind behaviorism. Choice *B*, Mary Ainsworth, was an American-Canadian psychologist known for work regarding emotional attachment in infants and the Strange Situation experiment. Choice *D*, Daniel Levinson, wrote *The Seasons of a Man's Life*, which suggested stages of development throughout the lifespan.

26. D: All of the above. Harlow, a theorist in mother-offspring attachment, noticed all of these qualities in monkeys who were given a wire mother substitute and were not shown warmth and affection. He theorized that newborns of many species, including humans, had an innate need to bond in this way in order to develop healthy personalities and attachment bonds.

Social and Cultural Diversity

This section covers concepts relating to societies and cultures. Important terms are provided in a glossary at the end of this section.

Cultures

Culture refers to the way a group of people lives, behaves, thinks, and believes. This can include behaviors, traditions, beliefs, opinions, values, religion, spirituality, communication, language, holidays, food, valued possessions, and family dynamics, among other factors. Geography, social status, economic standing, race, ethnicity, and religion can determine culture. Culture can be found within any organized community, such as in a place of worship or workplace. The following are examples of specific types of culture:

- Universal: the broadest category, also known as the human culture, and includes all people
- Ecological: groups created by physical location, climate, and geography
- National: patterns of culture for a specific country
- Regional: patterns for specific areas of a country that can include dialect, manners, customs and food/eating habits
- Racio-ethnic: group that shares common racial and ethnic background
- Ethnic: group that shares a common background, including religion and language

Biological and Social Factors

Biological and social factors influence a person's development and culture. Biological factors include genetics, such as the presence of any hereditary disorders, and phenotype, how the person looks and is perceived by others.

Social factors include the influence of parents, peers, and teachers. Socioeconomic status, immediate community, and society overall also influence the development of culture. The media impacts culture and can be a strong influence on social attitudes and behaviors. Specific occupations and types of employers have workplace cultures, which can affect workers positively or negatively.

Prejudice and Various "-isms"

Prejudice—the perceived opinions and beliefs that cause someone to feel or act in a negative manner toward a particular group—can present itself in a number of forms:

- Anti-Semitism: prejudice against the Jewish religion and culture
- Racism: prejudice against a particular race
- Sexism: prejudice against one or the other sex
- Ageism: prejudice against someone based on age, either young or old
- Classism: prejudice against someone based on his or her socio-economic class
- Ableism: prejudice against someone with disabilities or handicaps
- Homophobia: prejudice against the gay and lesbian community
- Transphobia: prejudice against the transgender community
- Nationalism: prejudice against non-natives in a specific country

Prejudice may also present itself as discrimination against someone due to immigrant status, national origin, religion, or weight.

Cultural Norms

Cultural norms refer to beliefs, attitudes, and values that are considered to be normal—i.e., consistent with the majority viewpoint—in a particular group. They shape the way the members of the group function and can be positive or negative in the eyes of other cultures.

Some cultures are considered tight, meaning they are quite regimented in their norms; this can be seen in societies where there is threat, such as war, an autocratic government system, or regular, formal rituals. Other cultures are considered loose, meaning they are more lax with their norms. These societies may seem disorganized or lacking values to outsiders.

Cultures can also reflect individualism or collectivism. Individualism focuses on each person, his or her individuality, and unique, personal rights. Collectivism focuses on the society as a whole and makes decisions to benefit all.

Culturally Different Clients

Clients may come from all backgrounds. It is important that counselors do not make any prior negative judgments regarding the personality or life of any client. Each individual has worth. It is essential for counselors to be mindful of any personal prejudices or biases and employ empathy and sensitivity when working with the client.

The client must be allowed to disclose details of a situation to determine influences from his or her culture. This can be done by conducting an interview with the client about his or her background, customs, personal beliefs, values, and relationships. Appropriate group interviews with key members in the client's life can also provide additional verbal and nonverbal information.

It is recommended that in order to be effective, counselors engage in ongoing professional development to gain skills and awareness of differing cultural needs and ethical standpoints and to ensure they are providing competent services. To maintain credibility and trust, counselors must honor the client's motives and goals for the session, taking into consideration cultural variations.

Acculturation, Assimilation, Cultural Encapsulation, and Worldview

Acculturation refers to the process of group-level change that can occur when two or more cultures meet. If this occurs with a smaller group and a larger group, the smaller group is usually—but not always—more likely to take on characteristics of the larger group.

Assimilation refers to the process of one or several people (not usually a large group) from a minority group accepting and modeling characteristics of a larger group or cultural setting.

Cultural encapsulation often refers to a narrowly held viewpoint, wherein the individual refuses to take into account other beliefs and cultures that differ. Many religious groups hold, or have held, these types of views in varying degrees. This often leads to preconceived notions, stereotyping, and other unsupported assumptions of others who may come from different backgrounds.

Worldview refers to the set of basic presuppositions that someone holds about the nature of reality, the world, culture, and society on a domestic and global scale. This view makes sense of the world around the individual and enables him or her to interpret life events and circumstances.

Women vs. Men in Counseling

Female and male clients may vary greatly on whether or not they seek counseling and on the goals they hope to achieve through counseling. Female clients are more likely to seek counseling. They may be more drawn to talking through problems to solve them and want to understand the process rather than merely focusing on a solution. They tend to rely more on intuition and are able to multi-task in their thought process. Female clients also tend to be more likely to express emotions. They are more likely to want to discuss life events that produced a strong emotional reaction in them in counseling sessions. In public, females often feel emotions are wrong or should be minimized, due to societal pressures. Some common issues women face include balancing a career and family, self-esteem, and mitigating societal expectations and pressures.

Men may feel distracted while trying to discuss a problem verbally, and these discussions may not bring the feelings of closeness and understanding that many women report experiencing. Men also typically prefer to discuss one problem and one component of that problem, at a time. While females are more likely to experience stronger emotions overall, men are more likely to experience stronger levels of anger and feel comfortable displaying anger publicly. Some common issues men face include work pressures, time commitment to family, work-life balance, and verbally expressing fears and concerns. It is important to note these are generalized tendencies between the two genders and not absolutes.

Some of these characteristics may certainly be seen in both genders or not at all. These differences also do not indicate that one way of approaching counseling is superior to another. In counseling sessions, it is important that counselors not attribute certain beliefs or approaches to a particular gender or to assume that one approach is more valuable than another. The practitioner must focus on interventions and resolutions that will support the goals of the client who is seeking treatment.

Class and Culture

Social class and culture influence each other. Class standing influences socioeconomic status, worldview, and personal values. Consequently, these affect the opportunities that might be available to someone in a particular class. Together, all of these aspects create variable cultures across social class strata.

Lower social classes may have less access to education, healthcare, or transportation. This may lead to placing more importance on getting a job for financial security as soon as possible, rather than paying money to attend college. Lower social class members may experience or instigate violence to procure resources. They may find more support in one another and have closer-knit communities if resources aren't available, such as trusting neighbors to watch children while they're working, rather than paying for childcare. Some studies have reported that members of lower-class neighborhoods tend to be more giving, but usually have poorer overall health outcomes. All of these factors describe the culture found within lower socio-economic classes.

Higher socio-economic classes may have more access to education, healthcare, and transportation, and usually do not have to rely on other people to meet their basic needs. With financial security, these members have the ability to focus on their needs and wants first. Their attitudes and beliefs tend to be somewhat entitled and less altruistic, and they are usually able to leverage their wealth to manage

problems. Thus, the availability of resources to a particular socio-economic class shapes their worldview. Collectively, this becomes the socio-economic group's culture.

IDEA

The Individuals with Disabilities Education Act (IDEA), enacted by Congress in 1975 and amended in 2004, legally ensures that children with disabilities from birth to age twenty-one have access to free individualized education plans, educational services that are appropriate for them, and minimally restrictive educational settings. IDEA protects the rights of parents and children and allows parents a voice in the educational decisions for their children.

Adults Over Sixty

As the average lifespan increases, older adults may become a larger proportion of counseling clientele. This demographic may seek counseling to discuss the diminished quality of life as they age, bereavement, transitioning to retirement, ageism (if they want or need to continue working), depression, or cognitive/physical decline. In counseling, older adults may present differently from younger clients in the sense that they are often learning to manage their reactions to personal events that are out of their control. Younger clients are often seeking direction regarding actions they can take to resolve a problem. It is important that counselors treat older adult clients as they would any other client, with respect and dignity, making sure to validate their feelings and support their goals for treatment.

ADA

Enacted by Congress, the Americans with Disabilities Act of 1990 (ADA) is a comprehensive civil rights legislation designed to protect individuals with disabilities from discriminatory practices, such as refusal of employment or lack of access to buildings. Disabilities covered under the act include mental and physical impairments that may limit normal activities. An individual considered a viable candidate for employment is one who can perform the necessary activities with reasonable accommodation. Consequently, the ADA requires all workplace and public entities to provide the necessary accommodations and structures for access, unless doing so places an unreasonable burden on the entity.

Older Workers

Older workers make up a larger part of the workforce than they have in the past. This may be due to a number of factors, such as recent economic downturns, increased lifespan, maintaining good health longer, and the desire to continue working.

However, some older workers may experience ageism as stereotypes and prejudices do exist toward older workers. These may include employers assuming that older workers may need extra accommodations to work, may not understand or want to work with new technologies, may be resistant to shifts in organizational and operational cultures, may require higher salaries, or may have health issues that lead to more absentee days or higher health insurance costs. Additionally, larger corporations often provide older workers with the option to retire if redundancies are looming, but this does not necessarily mean that older workers want to retire at this time.

Older workers may come to counselors for advice on how to handle these biases and concerns. As with all clients, it is important that counselors treat older workers with respect, listen to their desires for their

careers, and help them explore options that will satisfy these goals. These options may vary greatly, but might include things like teaching the older worker how best to market their skills to companies, fostering a sense of confidence and self-worth that is not solely based on employment, managing the mental and emotional adjustments to retirement, or directing clients to financial planning resources.

Alfred Adler's Concept of Birth Order

Alfred Adler believed that birth order, as well as other sibling contexts, played a major role in how an individual's personality was shaped. He attributed traits to each child relative to when they were born in comparison to their other living siblings, and he attributed traits to only children, twins, adopted children, and children born after the death of an older sibling.

Additionally, he felt that if all siblings were of the same gender, this context would hold a specific influence toward each sibling. Children who were the only gender among a group of siblings of the opposite gender (e.g., the only sister in a group of brothers) would be influenced by their sibling context as well.

Here's a table of some of the characteristics of birth order:

BIRTH POSITION	CHARACTERISTICS
OLDEST	Family places high expectations on the oldest child. Child is no longer the "only" child and must learn to share. Oldest child can become perfectionist and authoritative, yet can be helpful and learn to bear responsibility. The oldest child may find comfort in the father after birth of second child.
SECOND	In the family unit, the second child is constantly trying to compete with the first child. Second child is often rebellious and competitive, and tries to eclipse the older sibling.
MIDDLE	The middle child is "sandwiched" between the oldest and youngest child. The middle child may seek to please the parents through school or other talents in order to establish significance in the family unit. May have an easy-going personality.
YOUNGEST	The youngest child is nurtured by most members of the family, including other siblings. Youngest children may become dependent or spoiled due to their being the "baby" of the family.
ONLY	Only children are cherished by parents to the point of being over-protected. Only children may feel entitled to others' attention and may have a hard time sharing with others.
TWIN	Between the two, one twin may be stronger while the other is seen as "younger" or "weaker." One twin is likely to become the "leader" of the set. Identity issues may occur.
ADOPTED	Parents of an adopted child may spoil the child to make up for the loss of the biological parents. Child could grow to begrudge or glorify biological parents.
ONLY BOY AMONG GIRLS	Surrounded by women for much of the time. Boy may either 1) become the patriarch of the family or 2) exhibit feminine attributes.
ONLY GIRL AMONG BOYS	Surrounded by boys; brothers may be "protectors." Girl may either 1) become very feminine or 2) become a tomboy.
ALL BOYS	Growing up in an all-boys family, a child may be dressed as a girl if mothers' desire was for a girl. The child in question may accept given role or challenge it.
ALL GIRLS	Growing up in an all-girls family, child may be dressed as a boy. The child in question may accept given role or challenge it.

In these contexts, siblings' personalities will be shaped based on how they hope to best fit into their family and how they approach situations that they face within the family, as well as how they approach situations that the family faces as a unit. The parental roles can influence this process. In turn, this will affect how the individual later approaches life situations such as school, work, and interpersonal relationships.

Life Cycle of a Family

The life cycle of a family refers to the different stages of development through which a person progresses in relation to his or her family unit. As with other developmental stages, each holds potential obstacles that serve as the basis for skill building. The life cycle of a family is divided into five stages.

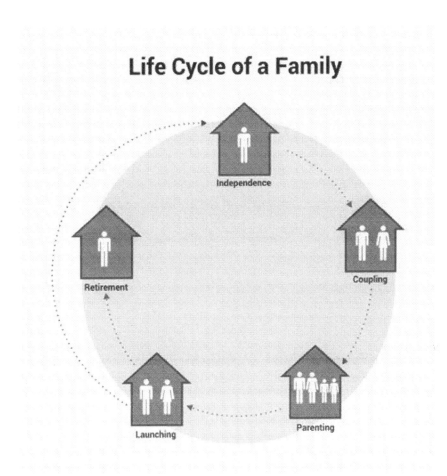

- Independence: individual leaves family unit into which he or she was born to establish economic and emotional independence

- Coupling: formation of a partnership with another individual to create and run a new family unit, work on professional paths, and learn how to manage household responsibilities, typically with no children

- Parenting: couple adding children to the family unit and raising them; involves sub-stages for each stage of childhood, from infancy to young adulthood, as each part of childhood presents its own challenges and rewards for the couple

- Launching adult children: children leaving the family unit to begin their own stages of independence; may initially still place some caretaking burden on the couple (e.g., paying for college or similar expenses), with the possibility that the couple experiences empty nest syndrome during this time

- Retirement: stage that typically consists of less caretaking of the needs of others (such as children's expenses), possibly less or no professional work, and aging

While the order of these stages typically remains consistent in the United States, the duration of each and the situations faced in a particular stage vary by culture, social status, race, and other demographic factors.

Culture or Ethnicity and Alternative Families

In the United States, a long-standing definition of the family unit has been the nuclear family, which consists of a single man and a single woman (typically married to one another) and their immediate children. However, there are other concepts of family reflected in other cultures that can encompass alternate dynamics.

Families can consist of any small group of individuals that are related by blood or choose to share their lives together. These can consist of heterosexual or homosexual couples with or without children, single parent households, childfree households, homes with extended family all living under one roof, blended families involving step-children and step-parents, or lifelong partners that choose not to marry legally.

Culture and ethnicity play a large role in defining a family unit. For example, many Eastern cultures value living with extended family and consider everyone in the physical household to be a member of the immediate family unit.

Theoretical Concepts of the Family Systems Theory

American psychiatrist Murray Bowen (1913–1990) first established the family systems theory, which later served as the basis for family, or systems-focused, counseling. The family systems theory seeks to explain the high level of emotional interdependence that family members have with one another, and how this interdependence individually affects each member of the family system. This theory states that the unique and complex cohesiveness that is found in family systems promotes positive behaviors like teamwork and taking care of one another; however, it can also cause negative behaviors, like anxiety or addictions, to diffuse from one person into the entire system.

The family systems theory is made up of eight distinct concepts:

- Triangles: refers to three-person systems, considered to be the smallest system that can still be stable. A third person adds extra support to manage intense emotions, tension, or conflict. The theory states that a two-person system cannot usually weather high levels of emotion, tension, or conflict over time.

- Differentiation of Self: how much an individual's personal beliefs differ from that of his or her group's beliefs. It is an important function of developing one's self. A strong self usually correlates with confidence and pragmatism, while a weak self usually correlates with an unhealthy need for approval from others.

- Nuclear Family Emotional System: referring to four different relationship patterns in this system. The patterns are marital conflict, dysfunction in one spouse, impairment in one or more children, and emotional distance, which refers to the fact that it occurs and how it affects the way problems are handled within the family.

- Family Projection Process: how parents project emotional conflict onto their children. The process can lead to pathologies in the child's psyche.

- Multigenerational Transmission Process: regarding the variance in differentiation of self between generations. The differentiation of self between parents and children over time leads to a widespread difference in beliefs between the oldest generation and the youngest generation of the family.

- Emotional Cutoff: regarding issue resolution. The act of failing to resolve issues between family members by reducing or eliminating contact with one another is emotional cut-off.

- Sibling Position: the importance of birth order and its influence on someone's functioning. It incorporates not only the birth order as it relates to how that person will function in workplaces and relationships, but also focuses on the birth order of each of the individual's parents and the influences those have on parenting styles.

- Societal Emotional Process: how the previous seven concepts hold true for any society. All families and societies will have progressive and regressive periods of development over time.

Important Terms

Affectional Orientation: a term used to describe one's romantic orientation toward a specific sex; an alternative term to *sexual orientation*

Alternative Family: any group of people that considers themselves a family unit but does not fall into the definition of a nuclear family

Emic: being aware of a client's culture and using counseling approaches accordingly

Empty Nest Syndrome: feelings of isolation, depression, or purposelessness that some parents may feel when their children move out of the family home

Ethnocentrism: a belief that one's culture is superior to another's

Ethnocide: purposely destroying another's ethnicity or culture

Ethnology: a branch of anthropology that systematically studies and compares the similarities and differences between cultures

Etic: an objective, universal viewpoint of clients

Gender Schema Theory: a theory by Sandra Bem in 1981 that describes how people in a society become gendered, especially through categories of information such as schemata

Heterogeneous Society: a society that is diverse in characteristics, cultural values, and language

High Context Culture: information is implicit and communicated through unspoken messages, with a focus on personal relationships and with fewer rules

Homogenous Society: a society that primarily consists of people with the same characteristics, cultural values, and language

Low Context Culture: information exchanged with little hidden meaning, with clear, explicit rules and standards, and relationships deemed less important than tasks

Modal Behavior: statistically, the most common and normative behaviors of a society

Nuclear Family: a family unit that consists of a married man and woman and their immediate children

Nuclear Family of Orientation: the family one is born into

Nuclear Family of Procreation: a family created by marriage and childbearing

Reciprocity: a social norm that says people should pay back what has been provided to them. This type of exchange relationship is used to build continuing relationships with others.

Sexual Orientation: an individual's sexual preference toward a specific gender

Stereotype: a preconceived notion about a group of people, not necessarily based in fact

Tripartite: awareness, knowledge, and skills of multicultural counseling

Practice Questions

1. On a neighborhood street, there are three houses. In one house lives a single father with two children. In another house, two same-sex partners live with their child and a dog. In the final house, a married heterosexual couple lives with their parents and grandparents. These three houses are comprised of what?
    a. Nuclear families
    b. Alternative families
    c. Child-focused families
    d. Standard families

2. Traditionally, a nuclear family consists of which of the following?
    a. One man, one woman, and their immediate children
    b. A single female head-of-household and her children
    c. A heterosexual or homosexual couple without any children
    d. Any type of family that has at least one domesticated pet

3. Sita's family lives in a large, multi-level home separated into different living suites. In addition to her parents and siblings, her maternal and paternal grandparents, aunts, uncles, and some cousins live there. The family follows the Hindu religion, spending one evening together each week in a designated prayer room. They eat traditional Indian foods and wear traditional Indian clothing most of the time. All of these details describe Sita's what?
    a. Religious views
    b. Acclimatization
    c. Need for alone time
    d. Culture

4. A human resources manager who only reviews applications from individuals that are between twenty-two and thirty years of age, regardless of any other credentials or experience, is demonstrating which of the following?
    a. Sexism
    b. Millennial-leaning bias
    c. Ageism
    d. Classism

5. Janna comes to the United States on a work visa after finishing college in her country of origin. She does very well in her job, and the company sponsors her for a permanent position. As years go by, she obtains a green card to continue living in the United States, begins to enjoy American sporting events, develops a strong grasp of Americans' usage of the English language and certain slang, and is known for hosting a spectacular 4th of July barbecue at her home every year. This case is an example of what?
    a. Assimilation
    b. Modeling
    c. Launching
    d. Acculturation

6. Which of the following stereotype(s) exist regarding older workers?
    a. The idea that that older workers will take more absentee and sick days
    b. The idea that older workers are resistant to new technology
    c. The idea that older workers are slower to learn new information
    d. All of the above

7. According to Murray Bowen's family systems theory, a strong sense of self is associated with
_____, while a weak sense of self is associated with _____.
    a. Confidence and pragmatism; seeking approval from others
    b. Only children; many siblings
    c. Authoritative parenting styles; laissez-faire parenting styles
    d. Physical strength; physical weakness

8. Who is associated with the concept of birth order and the influence that sibling position has on personality?
    a. Abraham Maslow
    b. Alfred Adler
    c. Albert Bandura
    d. Anna Freud

9. In which of the following stages of the family life cycle might parents experience "Empty Nest Syndrome"?
    a. Independence
    b. Parenting
    c. Launching adult children
    d. Retirement

10. According to Murray Bowen's family systems theory, the concept of the Nuclear Family Emotional System refers to four different relationship dynamics. These are which of the following?
    a. Conflict, distance, child-adult interactions, and proximity
    b. Marital conflict, dysfunction in one spouse, impairment in one or more children, and emotional distance
    c. Happy, conflicting, grieving, and joyous
    d. Parent-child conflict, spousal conflict, full family conflict, and sibling conflict

11. Sixteen-year-old Jake is at his great-grandfather's 95th birthday party. Jake is talking with his great-grandparents, grandparents, parents, and siblings. Jake's great-grandparents, who have been married for over seventy years, believe couples should stick it out no matter what. Jake and his siblings believe most people will divorce once in their lifetimes. The grandparents believe divorce can usually be avoided, and the parents believe divorce is sometimes necessary. This is an example of which concept of the Murray Bowen's family systems theory?
    a. Differentiation of Self
    b. Family Projection Process
    c. Multigenerational Transmission Process
    d. Emotional Cutoff

12. Which of the following often leads to preconceived notions, stereotyping, and unsupported assumptions of others who come from different backgrounds?
    a. Acculturation
    b. Assimilation
    c. Cultural encapsulation
    d. Worldview

13. A small healthcare clinic was recently acquired by a larger healthcare system. The small healthcare clinic began to follow the larger healthcare organization's efficient standard operating procedures, use their advanced appointment-scheduling software, and switch from a paper-based medical record system to the larger clinic's electronic medical record system. The employees of the small healthcare clinic also began to dress and act more formally at work. This process is an example of what?
    a. Acculturation
    b. Assimilation
    c. Cultural encapsulation
    d. Worldview

14. This federal law ensures that children with disabilities have access to free individualized education plans, educational services that are appropriate for them, and minimally restrictive educational settings.
    a. Individuals with Disabilities Education Act (IDEA)
    b. Americans with Disabilities Act (ADA)
    c. The Workforce Innovation and Opportunity Act
    d. 1994 School-to-Work Opportunities Act

15. The statistically most common and normative behaviors of a society are referred to as what?
    a. Culture
    b. Modal behavior
    c. Tripartite
    d. Ethnology

16. What are some specific issues cited as commonly discussed by women in counseling?
    a. Infertility, marital conflict, and eating disorders
    b. Balancing a career and family, self-esteem, and mitigating societal expectations/pressures
    c. Exhaustion, joint pain, and postpartum depression
    d. Anxiety, work-life balance, and finances

17. Higher-class members tend to have more access to _____, while lower-class members tend to be more _____ in nature.
    a. Dining out and cultural shows; homebodies
    b. Community and family; aloof and solitary
    c. Education and healthcare; altruistic and social
    d. Food and water; hungry and thirsty

18. Which of the following refers to the perspective someone holds about society on a domestic and global scale?
    a. Worldview
    b. Cultural Encapsulation
    c. Ethnicity
    d. Ethnocentrism

19. A large, multi-story building that serves as the primary office for a business corporation in the United States only has stairs available to access each floor and the main front door. There are no elevators within in the building, and there is no ramp anywhere outside of any of the external doors. Additionally, all of the doors that lead into the building are revolving doors, which the corporation cites as being more energy-efficient. This organization is in direct violation of _____.
 a. Individuals with Disabilities Education Act (IDEA)
 b. Americans with Disabilities Act of 1990 (ADA)
 c. Workforce Innovation and Opportunity Act
 d. The Hidden Job Market

20. A practitioner is reviewing her appointment schedule and notices that her next client has a traditional Chinese name. The practitioner should assume _____.
 a. That the office translator will need to be present for the session and should be summoned immediately in order to ensure the client's comfort
 b. That the client is an only child
 c. That the client is male
 d. Nothing

21. In many Middle Eastern countries, conservative dress is seen and preferred by most constituents. In many European countries, trending fashion is preferred and enjoyed by most constituents. In many beach climates, most constituents prefer very casual attire. Dress preferences listed here are an example of what?
 a. Trends that change
 b. Cultural norms
 c. Political ideology
 d. Peer pressure

22. A small country like Denmark—where most people hold the same cultural beliefs, education status, dress, and traditions—is considered a/an _____; a larger country like the United States—where people come from many diverse backgrounds and many have emigrated from other countries—is considered a/an_____.
 a. Narrow country; broad country
 b. Ethnography; demography
 c. Homogenous society; heterogeneous society
 d. Heterogeneous society; homogenous society

23. Some issues that adults over sixty face and may want to discuss in counseling include what?
 a. Bereavement, ageism in the workforce, and unemployment
 b. The Millennial generation, religion, and politics
 c. Sagging skin, hair loss, and cancer
 d. None of the above

24. According to Murray Bowen's family systems theory, the smallest system unit that can still be stable consists of at least _____ entities.
 a. Two
 b. Three
 c. Four
 d. Five

Answer Explanations

1. B: Alternative families. These families consist of any group of people who, due to blood relation or by choice, choose to live together and support one another as a familial unit. Choice *A*, nuclear families, are families that consist of a couple and their dependent children. Choices *C* and *D* are not actual terms for describing types of families.

2. A: One man, one woman, and their immediate children. Nuclear family is a term that is widely considered to be narrow in its definition of a family unit. The other family types listed are examples of alternative families.

3. D: Culture. All of the details provided about Sita's family provide insight to their collective values, beliefs, traditions, and practices. Choice *A* is incorrect, although religious views are part of cultural values and practices. Choice *B*, acclimatization, is the ability to adjust to a change in the environment. Choice *C*, need for alone time, may be a result of living in a large household, but it is not the best answer to this question.

4. C: Ageism. Ageism is discrimination against someone because of his or her age. In this situation, the manager is automatically filtering out older applicants even if they bring appropriate skills and knowledge for the position, simply because of age. Choice *A*, sexism, is when prejudice or discrimination is shown against someone on the basis of sex. Choice *B*, millennial-leaning bias is not an actual term. Choice *D*, classism, is prejudice against someone because of a certain socioeconomic class.

5. A: Assimilation. Assimilation refers to the process one or several people undertake when moving into a new culture and adopting the new culture's traditions. Janna adopted completely new, traditional American practices and celebrations after immigrating to the United States. Choice *B*, modeling, refers to when a counselor models a behavior for a client in the hopes that the client will start to mimic that behavior. Choice *C*, launching, is a phase in the life cycle of a family where children leave the family unit in order to begin their own stages of independence. Choice *D*, acculturation, is the process of group-level change that can occur when two or more cultures meet.

6. D: All of the above. These stereotypes are a form of ageism that exist toward older workers. These ideas include that older workers may need extra accommodations to work, may not understand new technologies, or may have health issues that lead to more absentee days or higher health insurance costs.

7. A: Confidence and pragmatism; seeking approval from others. Bowen discusses this idea under the concept of "Differentiation of Self." This refers to how much an individual's personal beliefs differ from that of his or her group's beliefs and plays an important role in whether someone develops a strong or weak sense of self.

8. B: Alfred Adler. Adler believed that birth position and the context of one's sibling relationships played a pivotal role in shaping one's personality. Choice *A*, Abraham Maslow, created Maslow's Hierarchy of Needs, a pyramid that depicts biological and psychological needs. Choice *C*, Albert Bandura, was a psychologist who theorized that learning takes place socially through observation and imitation of others and that not all behaviors are conditioned. Choice *D*, Anna Freud, was a psychoanalyst that focused on the ego and child development.

9. C: Launching adult children. Empty nest syndrome is characterized by feelings of sadness and purposelessness that parents may feel when their children leave the family home and begin adult independence. Choice *A*, independence, occurs when the individual leaves the family unit into which he or she was born to establish independence. Choice *B*, parenting, is when a couple adds children to the family unit and raises them. Choice *D*, retirement, is the stage that focuses less on caretaking and professional work.

10. B: Marital conflict, dysfunction in one spouse, impairment in one or more children, and emotional distance. These four dynamics refer to four different relationship patterns in the Nuclear Family Emotional System, and they affect how family units handle various problems.

11. C: Multigenerational Transmission Process. This concept explains how the variance in differentiation of self between parents and children over time leads to a widespread difference in beliefs between the oldest generation and the youngest generation of the family. Choice *A* is incorrect; differentiation of self refers to how much an individual's personal beliefs differ from that of his or her group's beliefs, and Jake is identifying with his peers here. Choice *B* is incorrect; family projection process refers to how parents project emotional conflict onto their children. Choice *D* is incorrect; emotional cutoff is the act of failing to resolve issues between family members by reducing or eliminating contact with one another.

12. C: Cultural encapsulation. This refers to a narrow viewpoint of global cultures or any culture differing from one's own. Choice *A*, acculturation, refers to the process of group-level change that can occur when two or more cultures meet. Choice *B*, assimilation, refers to the process of one or several people from a minority group accepting and modeling characteristics of a larger group. Choice *D*, worldview, refers to the set of basic presuppositions that someone holds about the nature of reality, the world, culture and society on a domestic and global scale.

13. A: Acculturation. This process describes how a smaller culture tends to adopt the practices of a larger culture when the two cultures meet. In this situation, the smaller clinic began to adopt the more formal, advanced culture of the larger system. Choice *B*, assimilation, refers to the process of one or several people from a minority group accepting and modeling characteristics of a larger group. Choice *C*, cultural encapsulation, refers to a viewpoint wherein the individual refuses to take into account other beliefs and cultures that differ. Choice *D*, worldview, refers to the set of basic presuppositions that someone holds about the nature of reality, culture, and society.

14. A: Individuals with Disabilities Education Act (IDEA). This law was enacted in 1975 and also provides communities with extra funding to provide resources for disabled children. Choice *B*, the Americans with Disabilities Act, is legislation designed to protect individuals with disabilities from discriminatory practices. Choice *C*, the Workforce Innovation and Opportunity Act, is designed to streamline training programs in the workforce. Choice *D*, 1994 School-to-Work Opportunities Act, is a federal act designed to support education at the state level.

15. B: Modal behavior. Similar to the term *mode*, which indicates the number that occurs the most often in a dataset, modal behavior describes behaviors that occur most often within a group of people. Choice *A*, culture, refers to the beliefs, customs, and arts of a particular people. Choice *C*, tripartite, refers to awareness, knowledge, and skills of multicultural counseling. Choice *D*, ethnology, is a branch of anthropology that systematically studies and compares the similarities and differences between cultures.

16. B: Balancing a career and family, self-esteem, and mitigating societal expectations/pressures. Men, on the other hand, are more likely to discuss work pressures, time commitment to family, work-life balance, and verbally expressing fears and concerns.

17. C: Education and healthcare; altruistic and social. Higher-class members often have enough money to pay for services and tend to keep to themselves; lower-class members form communities they rely upon, and studies indicate that they are more giving.

18. A: Worldview. One's worldview is typically comprised of personal beliefs, values, and attitudes about the world around them and beyond. Choice *B*, cultural encapsulation, refers to a viewpoint wherein the individual refuses to take into account other beliefs and cultures that differ. Choice *C*, ethnicity, is belonging to a certain group that has a common cultural tradition. Choice *D*, ethnocentrism, is a belief that one's culture is superior to another's.

19. B: Americans with Disabilities Act of 1990 (ADA). This law requires that workplaces in the United States provide the necessary accommodations and structures for access, unless doing so places an unreasonable burden on the entity. In the building above, there are no accommodations for individuals with physical handicaps to enter the building or access any offices. Choice *A*, Individuals with Disabilities Education Act, was enacted in 1975 and also provides communities with extra funding to provide resources for disabled children. Choice *C*, Workforce Innovation and Opportunity Act, is designed to streamline training programs in the workforce. Choice *D*, the Hidden Job Market, is a term used for jobs that aren't advertised.

20. D: Nothing. Practitioners will serve clients from all backgrounds and should not make any assumptions from intake information. Practitioners should be aware of any personal biases they may hold and make all inferences about the client's situation from information that comes directly from their sessions.

21. B: Cultural norms. Cultural norms refer to beliefs, attitudes, and values that are considered to be normal, or the majority viewpoint, in a particular group. They can be quite strict in some cultures and quite lax in others.

22. C: Homogenous society; heterogeneous society. A homogenous society is one where the people are very similar in background, attitudes, and beliefs; a heterogeneous society embodies a great deal of diversity within its people.

23. A: Bereavement, ageism in the workforce, and unemployment. These are some issues older adults face and report discussing in counseling as they begin to lose friends and family, or if they are forced into retirement or made redundant in their workplace.

24. B: Three. According to the concept of Triangles in the family systems theory, a third person adds an extra support to manage intense emotions, tension, or conflict. The theory states that a two-person system cannot usually weather high levels of emotion, tension, or conflict over time.

Counseling and Helping Relationships

Building Counselor and Client Relationships

Creating rapport with clients requires counselors to engage in specific approaches using appropriate therapeutic techniques. In addition to the use of theory, they must convey a genuine attitude of empathy and respect for their clients. Using positive regard, as well as a nonjudgmental style, is essential to creating a sense of comfort and willingness for clients to open up to their counselor. Counselors should carefully evaluate each client and develop a plan for services that will best meet his or her needs. The plan should be communicated and agreed upon with the clients, ensuring that they feel the counselor is trustworthy and competent.

Person-Centered Approach

Carl Rogers developed the person-centered, or humanistic, approach to counseling, which stressed the importance of the counseling relationship, as well as the need to evaluate therapy for effectiveness. Rogers believed that three core conditions must exist for therapy to facilitate change: empathy, positive regard, and congruence. Rogers's work was continued by Robert Carkhuff, who created a five-point scale to measure the core conditions and effectiveness of a counselor. This scale attempts to measure the degree to which the counselor is providing effective levels of empathy, genuineness, concreteness, and respect.

- Level 1. Therapist is contradictory in statements and nonverbal cues and exhibits defensiveness.
- Level 2. Therapist is superficially professional but lacks genuineness.
- Level 3. Therapist does not express defensiveness; there is implied but not overt professionalism.
- Level 4. Therapist is genuine and nondefensive.
- Level 5. Therapist is open and honest and accurately and genuinely reflects ideas and reactions to client.

In his 1967 book, *Toward Effective Counseling and Psychotherapy*, Carkhuff found that therapeutic interventions did not always have a long-term positive impact, and in some cases, clients worsened after counseling. Carkhuff's findings were summarized in a famous quote that "therapy may be for better or for worse." This led him to conduct further research on specific attributes of the counselor that contributed to successful outcomes.

Additional Counseling Skills

The following are additional counseling skills:

- Restatement: clarification through repeating back the client's words, as understood by the counselor

- Reflection: restatement of what the counselor heard from the client, emphasizing any underlying emotional content (can be termed *reflection of feeling*)

- Paraphrasing: repeating back a client's story while providing an empathic response

- Summarizing: reiteration of the major points of the counseling discussion

- Silence: moments during which neither the client nor the counselor speak; can be used for reflection but may indicate resistance from the client

- Confrontation: technique in which the counselor identifies discrepancies from the client in a supportive manner (counselor may also ask for clarification to determine if content was misheard prior to exposing possible inconsistencies)

- Structuring: used to set goals and agree upon plan for counseling; also used within sessions to make effective use of time and respect boundaries

Five Tasks of Healthy Individuals

To assist individuals in achieving wellness, it is essential for counselors to understand all facets and influences on well-being. The World Health Organization initially defined well-being as physical, social, and mental wellness, along with the absence of disease. This idea was expanded by Myers, Witmer, and Sweeney, who created the Wheel of Wellness concept in an attempt to understand and classify the "whole" person. The Wheel of Wellness illustrates five life tasks, which include essence or spirituality, work and leisure, friendship, love, and self-direction. Self-direction contains twelve subtasks: *sense of worth, sense of control, realistic beliefs, emotional awareness and management, problem solving and creativity, sense of humor, nutrition, exercise, self-care, stress management, gender identity,* and *cultural identity*.

Motives for Helping Others Through Counseling

Just as clients are motivated to seek counseling to resolve issues and/or improve their lives, counselors exhibit motivation to help others. Counseling, as a profession, allows an opportunity to positively impact the lives of individuals and help improve society. It is important as part of professional development for counselors to explore their motivation to join the profession. Some graduate programs may require individuals to receive counseling as part of their education to ensure they have adequately addressed their own issues and prevent using the clients to get their own needs met. In some specific areas of counseling, such as addictions, it is more common for counselors to have experienced addiction and recovered, thus motivating them to assist others.

Coping Skills

Teaching coping skills is an important role of the counselor in the therapeutic relationship. Coping skills enable individuals to manage stressful situations, solve problems, handle uncertainty, and develop resilience. Coping skills can include solution-focused problem solving, removing negative self-talk, learning mindfulness or other stress management techniques, and gaining support through friends, family, and community. Individuals may learn how to identify specific patterns to their feelings and behaviors, and thus, learn new and healthier responses. As there are many ways for individuals to develop and practice coping skills, counselors can provide options and unique plans for clients to best meet their needs.

Empathy

Empathy is considered an essential counseling skill. It is used not only to initially build trust but also throughout the counseling process. The process of empathy is used to help the counselor understand the client's viewpoint. It is more complex than sympathy, which is somewhat passive and a sense of feeling bad for another person. Empathy focuses on gaining insight into the client's experience to offer effective means to deal with any issues or concerns. Although psychologist Edward Titchener was the first to use the term, it is strongly associated with the client-centered approach of Carl Rogers. Rogers believed empathy extended beyond understanding a person's situation; it involved the counselor imagining him or herself in that situation. This level of empathy requires genuineness, acceptance, and a small measure of vulnerability on the part of the counselor.

Cultural Awareness

Counselors must be adept at working with diverse populations. Diversity includes race, culture, gender, ethnicity, sexual orientation, socioeconomic status, religion, and age. As part of the profession, counselors will provide services to individuals and families with whom they have no cultural similarity. Thus, it is essential for counselors to develop and maintain a level of cultural competence. The first step is for them to engage in self-awareness and gain an understanding of their own identity, including their belief systems and biases. As part of the counseling process, counselors should be able to acknowledge differences and communicate to clients with trust and credibility while demonstrating mutual respect. They should engage in ongoing professional development, both to gain skills and awareness of differing cultural needs, as well as from an ethical standpoint to ensure they are providing competent services. To maintain credibility and trust, counselors must clearly define issues and goals for counseling, taking into consideration cultural variations.

Initial Phase of Relationship Building

At the onset of the process, the counselor and client will progress through the relationship phase, which has four specific phases. These phases may be completed at a varying pace, depending on both parties. Some phases can be completed quickly, while others may take several sessions.

- Phase 1. Initiation, or entry phase: This is the introduction to the counseling process, which sets the stage for the development of the client/counselor relationship.

- Phase 2. Clarification phase: This phase defines the problem and need for the therapeutic relationship.

- Phase 3. Structure phase: The counselor defines the specifics of the relationship, its intended outcomes, and responsibilities of both parties.

- Phase 4. Relationship phase: The client and counselor have developed a relationship and will work toward mutually agreed-upon goals.

Stages of Positive Interaction

Once a working relationship is established, the client and counselor will need to develop and maintain positive interactions to ensure the effectiveness of counseling. Positive interactions ensure the

therapeutic relationship advances and supports clients in meeting their goals. The counseling relationship has four stages.

- Stage 1. Exploration of feelings and definition of problem: Counselors will use rapport-building skills, define the structure of the counseling process and relationship, and work with their clients on goal setting.

- Stage 2. Consolidation: This is the process of the clients integrating the information and guidance from the counselor, allowing them to gain additional coping skills and identify alternate ways to solve problems.

- Stage 3. Planning: During this phase, clients can begin employing techniques learned in counseling and prepare to manage on their own.

- Stage 4. Termination: This is the ending of the therapeutic relationship, when clients feel equipped to manage problems independently and have fully integrated techniques learned in counseling.

Silence

Silence can be an effective skill in therapy but must be used carefully, especially in the early stages of the process. Initially, clients may be silent due to many factors, such as fear, resistance, discomfort with opening up, or uncertainty about the process. Counselors who use silence in initial sessions must ensure clients do not perceive the counselor as bored, hostile, or indifferent. As counseling progresses, clients may gain additional comfort with silence and use it as a way to reflect on content, process information, consider options, and gain self-awareness. Newer counselors may have more difficulty with silence, as they may believe they are not being helpful if they are not talking. Silence is also viewed differently by culture, so cultural awareness is important in understanding and using it as a therapeutic tool.

Transference

Transference is a concept from psychoanalysis that refers to the process of the clients transferring any feelings toward others onto the counselor. These feelings are likely unconscious, as they arrive from childhood experiences and relationships. For example, the counselor may remind clients of their distant parent, and the clients will project feelings about that parent onto the counselor. Transference can be very powerful, although both positive and negative forms exist. Positive or good transference allows clients to work through issues with the counselor, who is safe and nonreactive. Clients can project negative feelings or emotions onto the counselor, thus being able to resolve them in the absence of the parent or individual. Negative or bad transference exists when clients project negative emotions and become angry or hostile toward the counselor. This type of transference can create a blockage and diminish the effectiveness of therapy. It is the role of the counselor to understand and manage transference as it arises in the relationship. Transference can also occur for the counselor with clients. Supervision and consultation are both helpful and necessary should this occur.

Attending

Attending is the act of the counselor giving clients his or her full attention. Attending to the client shows respect for their needs, can encourage openness, and can create a sense of comfort and support in the counseling process. There are several ways for counselors to attend actively to clients, including maintaining appropriate eye contact, using reassuring body language and gestures, and monitoring their

tone and expressions. Counselors can communicate support and a nonjudgmental attitude through an open posture and eye gaze that shows interest but not intimidation. They should use a caring verbal tone and facial expressions, which indicate attention to what their clients are saying, and can be used in addition to silence to create a positive environment for counseling.

Client Resistance

Resistance to counseling, at some point, may be unavoidable. The process of change is difficult, and clients may become overtly or unconsciously oppositional when faced with the need to adjust thoughts or behaviors. In psychoanalytic terms, clients are resistant in an attempt to avoid anxiety brought up through the counseling process. Resistance can be very obvious, such as canceling or delaying appointments, not following through, or not fully engaging in the process. Resistance can also be subtler; clients can display resistance through disinterest or noncompliance. The counselor can contribute to client resistance through inadequate therapeutic interventions, such as having an agenda that does not meet clients' needs. Although resistance can interfere with the process, it can also be very powerful when dealt with effectively. Counselors need to pay close attention to resistance, understand its origins, and work to help clients recognize and work through blockages.

Questions

As part of any counseling session, counselors will ask both open and closed questions. Open questions are more likely to provide helpful information, as they require the client to express feelings, beliefs, and ideas. Open questions often begin with "why," "how," or "when" or "tell me …". Closed questions may be less helpful, as they may elicit brief responses of one or few words.

Counselors do need to be aware of the limitations of asking questions. Any questions asked should have purpose and provide information that will be meaningful to the counselor and the relationship. Curiosity questions should be avoided, as well as asking too many questions, which may feel interrogating to the client. A counselor can ask follow-up questions for clarification as needed. The counselor should provide the client adequate time to answer questions and elaborate but also allow time for the client to talk freely.

Reflecting

Reflecting is a basic counseling skill designed to build rapport and help clients become aware of underlying emotions. Counselors "reflect back" what a client says, both to indicate they are attending and also to analyze and interpret meanings. Reflecting is more than simply paraphrasing a client's words, as it involves more in-depth understanding and an attempt to elicit further information. An example would be a client stating, "I'm not sure what to do about my current relationship. I can't decide if I should stay or leave." The counselor would reflect by stating, "It sounds like you are conflicted about what to do; this is a difficult decision to make," and follow up with a probing question or time for the client to process and react.

Errors

Reflecting is one of several active listening and rapport-building skills but should not be overused. It is essential that the counselor be able to offer back meaningful restatements and not simply repeat back what is heard. It is also important that the counselor accurately reflects any feeling and does not project or misinterpret. In some cases, misinterpretation can help the client further clarify and is not

detrimental to the relationship. By using reflection and clarification, any errors can be corrected. Even when errors occur, when the counselor clarifies what the client means, it communicates that the counselor is invested in understanding the client. From a cultural awareness standpoint, the counselor should be sensitive to any differences and ensure there is a level of trust prior to engaging in more in-depth reflection.

Guidelines for Giving Advice

There are two main types of advice: substantive and process. Substantive advice can be considered directive and may involve the counselor imposing his or her opinions onto clients. Process advice is more empowering and helps clients navigate options for solving their own issues. An example would be a client who is struggling with anxiety. Substantive advice would be the counselor telling the client he or she should practice deep breathing. Process advice, in the same example, would be teaching the client how relaxation techniques can lessen anxiety and providing examples. Counselors can offer process advice to help clients better understand their problems and possible solutions. Clients may ask for advice, and in some situations, it may be appropriate for the counselor to offer process advice; it is less likely that substantive advice should be given. Providing counseling is more complex than simply giving advice; thus, counselors should explore when, why, and how to give advice, if needed. As the goal of counseling is to help individuals gain a better self-awareness and competence, giving advice may undermine the process by not allowing clients an opportunity to learn ways to solve their own issues both within and after counseling.

Summarizing

Summarizing is another active listening and rapport-building technique. The counselor listens to the content provided by the clients and summarizes the essential points of the conversation. This process can help isolate and clarify the essential aspects of issues and ensure that both the client and the counselor can focus on the most critical tasks. Additionally, summarization can be helpful in goal setting or at the end of a session.

Phases of a Crisis Period

In 1964, psychiatry professor Gerald Caplan defined the recognizable phases of a crisis:

- Phase 1. This first phase consists of the initial threat or event, which triggers a response. The individual may be able to employ coping skills or defense mechanisms to avoid a crisis.

- Phase 2. This second phase is the escalation, during which initial attempts to manage the crisis are ineffective and the individual begins to experience increased distress.

- Phase 3. The third phase is the acute crisis phase, during which anxiety continues and may intensify to panic or a fight-or-flight response. There are still attempts to problem-solve during this phase, and new tactics may be used.

- Phase 4. The fourth phase is the climax of the crisis when solutions have failed; the individual may experience personality disorganization and become severely depressed, violent, and possibly suicidal.

Crisis Intervention

A crisis situation requires swift action and specially trained mental health personnel and can occur at any time in any setting. Albert Roberts proposed a seven-stage model to deal with a crisis and provide effective intervention and support. Roberts's stages are as follows:

- Stage 1. Conduct thorough biopsychosocial assessments of client functioning, and identify any imminent danger to self or others.

- Stage 2. Make contact, and quickly establish rapport; it is important that the counselor is accepting, nonjudgmental, flexible, and supportive.

- Stage 3. Identify specific problems and the possible cause of crisis; begin to prioritize the specific aspect of the problem most in need of a solution.

- Stage 4. Provide counseling in an attempt to understand the emotional content of the situation.

- Stage 5. Work on coping strategies and alternative solutions, which can be very challenging for an individual in crisis.

- Stage 6. Implement an action plan for treatment, which could include therapy, the 12-step program, hospitalization, or social services support.

- Stage 7. Follow up, and continue to evaluate status; ensure that the treatment plan is effective, and make adjustments as needed.

Critical Incident Stress Debriefing

Designed to support individuals after a traumatic event, Critical Incident Stress Debriefing (CISD) is a structured form of crisis management. Specifically, it is short-term work done in small groups but is not considered psychotherapy. Techniques used include processing, defusing, ventilating, and validating thoughts, experiences, feeling and emotions. CISD is best for secondary trauma victims, not primary trauma victims. For example, in cases of workplace violence, any employees who witnessed an event or who were indirectly impacted could benefit from CISD. Employees who were first-degree victims would need more individualized, specialized care and therapeutic intervention. It is important that CISD is offered as quickly as possible after an event; research has indicated it is most effective within a 24- to 72-hour time frame and becomes less effective the more time lapses after the event. CISD can be managed by specially trained personnel and could include mental health workers, medical staff, human resources, or other professionals. Trained Crisis Response Teams can be ready or quickly available to provide support directly following a traumatic situation.

Support

Support is a broad term for the way in which a counselor provides assistance and care to clients. Nonjudgmental support helps clients to open up, identify issues and the need for counseling, and set personal goals. A counselor can support a client by providing reassurance, acting as a sounding board, and simply listening without reaction. For the client, support from the counselor can allow a sense of being temporarily unburdened, which can facilitate healing. Support groups allow for peers or individuals experiencing similar issues (such as single parents and those struggling with addiction or eating disorders) to provide companionship and comfort through shared experiences.

Grief

Grief is the emotional reaction to any type of loss. Emotions can range from sadness to despair, anger, or guilt. A loss could include a person, pet, job, or relationship. Bereavement is grief specific to the loss of a loved one. Although individuals can experience a range of emotions, there are two types of grieving. Instrumental grieving is considered more cognitive and focuses on managing emotional reactions and problem solving. It is more *thinking* than *feeling* and is considered a masculine way of dealing with grief. Intuitive grieving is more *feeling* than *thinking*. It is thought to be a more feminine way of grieving and focuses on expressing feelings, sharing, and processing emotions. Elisabeth Kubler-Ross developed the most well-known model for grief in 1969. The five-phase model suggests that individuals pass through at least two of five linear stages: denial, anger, bargaining, depression, and finally, acceptance. Individuals can also cycle back through certain stages.

Counselors can assist clients in dealing with grief by providing support and helping them process emotions and develop skills to adjust to life after a loss. It is important for counselors to understand that individuals experience grief in unique ways and to recognize when grief becomes unmanageable and can lead to more serious concerns, such as depression.

Reassurance

Reassurance is an affirming therapeutic technique used to encourage and support clients. Reassurance can help alleviate doubts and increase confidence. Counselors use reassurance when a client experiences setbacks or an inability to recognize progress. Clients can be reminded of past successes to help bolster their ability to solve current problems. It is important that reassurance is genuine and not overused by counselors to pacify clients, but rather as a tool to validate and inspire continued growth.

Promoting Relaxation

As part of the counseling process, clients may need to learn basic relaxation techniques, which can be simple to learn and practice. Stress can cause increased anxiety and tension; thus, relaxation techniques help reduce both mental and physical stress. Clients may present with racing thoughts, fatigue, or headaches; techniques such as awareness, breath work, and progressive relaxation can be of great benefit. Clients who have a reduction in their stress level may be more engaged in the counseling process and better able to manage difficulties outside of sessions. Meditation is a powerful relaxation tool to help build awareness and the ability to calm oneself. Relaxation can help diminish the activity of stress hormones in the body, reduce feelings of anger and frustration, lower heart rate, and improve confidence.

Making Referrals

In some cases, a client may require specialized service that is out of the scope of the counselor. At these times, a counselor may need to refer the client to another professional. It is important that the counselor is familiar with community resources and any specialized care a client may need. It is also essential to discuss with the client why a referral is recommended and ensure the client is comfortable with the decision and understands next steps. The counselor must be familiar with ethical guidelines surrounding referrals and not refer out simply due to discomfort with or dislike for a client. A counselor who refers out for such personal reasons risks clients feeling abandoned, and the ACA Code of Ethics states that the needs of the clients must be put before those of the counselor. In these situations, the

counselor should seek supervision and consultation regarding his or her personal issues. If the counselor is unable to provide appropriate care, then the client should be referred out.

Goals

Setting goals is an important aspect of the therapeutic process. Talk therapy may seem unstructured or capable of lasting for long periods of time; however, both the client and the counselor are responsible for setting and working toward measurable change. Goals of counseling can include the desire for physical change, such as getting into shape or losing weight, and career aspirations and/or social goals, such as gaining increased support or modifying relationships. Other types of goals can include emotional, spiritual, and intellectual. Goals can be immediate, short term, or long term, and clients may want to achieve several goals at different paces. Goals can take the form of SMART goals, which are specific, measurable, achievable, relevant, and time-bound. Specific means detailing why you want to accomplish the goal, what specifically there is to accomplish, who is involved, the setting for the goal, and what kind of resources are involved. Measurable means designating a system of tracking your goals in order to stay motivated. Achievable is making sure that the goal is realistic, like looking at financial factors or other limitations. Relevant means making sure it's the right time for the goal, if it matches your needs, or if the goal seems worthwhile to pursue. Finally, time-bound is developing a target date so that there is a clear deadline to focus on.

Flaws in Goal Setting

Goal setting must be specific to each client and should be mutually agreed upon. Setting clear time frames, supported by the counselor, is essential to success. Goal setting may cause issues if goals are too ambitious or vague or have no identifiable benefit. It is also important to explore what motivation exists for a client to work toward a goal. If adequate motivation is present, the counselor also needs to consider what will happen if the goal is not met. In some cases, failure to meet goals can cause a client to become highly discouraged and unwilling to stick with the process of reformulating goals. During the process of working toward goals, a client may realize another goal is better suited. It's important to reevaluate goals during the process to help the client grow and embrace personal change.

Rational Problem-Solving Process

Rational problem solving is based on facts and clear consequences. It is an analytical approach that relies on predictability and understood outcomes. The rational decision-making process has distinct steps to define a problem and then weigh and rank the decision-making criteria. Next, the client must develop, evaluate, and select the best alternative. It is also important to explore consequences as well as what might happen if no decision is made and no action is taken.

Intuitive Problem Solving

Intuitive problem solving is based on feelings and instinct. It is an approach based on emotions and a "gut feeling" about what might be the right decision. Although in some cases it may be the right way and result in the correct decision, it is important for the counselor and client to work together on understanding any problem and possible solutions. It is also important to know when to utilize rational decision making versus intuitive or when to employ both strategies.

Modeling

Modeling is a technique used in therapy to allow clients to learn healthy and appropriate behaviors. Counselors "model" certain actions and attitudes, which can teach a client to behave in a similar fashion in his or her own life. Modeling is somewhat indirect. It is not suggested to the client to act in specific ways; rather, the counselor demonstrates desired behaviors, and the client begins imitating them.

Reinforcement When Analyzing Behavior

Reinforcement is a tool of behavior modification, used to either encourage or discourage specific thoughts or behaviors. Positive reinforcement rewards desired behaviors, thus encouraging the client to continue them. Counselors can provide positive verbal reinforcements, for example, to a client sharing difficult feelings, which in turn will encourage the client to continue sharing. The term *positive* in this case does not refer to a "good" outcome but to the act of applying a reward, such as a positive reaction from the counselor. Negative reinforcement works to discourage unwanted thoughts or behaviors by removing a stimulus after a specific action. The negative does not make it "bad"—rather, it is the act of removing a negative stimulus to eliminate a specific thought or behavior.

Extinguishing

Extinguishing is the process of ending, or making extinct, a specific maladaptive thought pattern or behavior. Previously occurring behaviors were reinforced, and when reinforcement (either positive or negative) ceases, the behavior will eventually be extinguished. It may be a goal in counseling to extinguish unwanted thoughts or behaviors that are harmful or a hindrance to the client.

Contract

As part of the intake process, counselors may wish to develop and agree upon a contract with the client. Contracts outline goals and responsibilities of both parties and may help to alleviate potential miscommunication. Important components of a contract include an outline of the service being provided, a description of the counselor's qualifications, and any explanation of the scope of practice. A clause outlining client rights and confidentiality should be included. Lastly, the counselor may wish to include specifics about session time, fees, and consequences of a client being late, missing, or canceling sessions. Contracts can serve to empower clients by clarifying service and allowing clients to take an active role in their therapeutic care. They may also be flexible, allowing either party to modify the contract as needed.

In-Life Desensitization

Desensitization is a behavior modification technique designed to replace an anxiety-producing stimulus with a relaxation response. Also known as systematic desensitization, it is a process to help the client manage fear or phobias. The client is taught relaxation techniques, which can include breathing, mindfulness, and muscle relaxation. Next, a "fear hierarchy" is created to rank stimulus from least to most fearful. The client is gradually exposed to the object or action that causes anxiety and then moves up the fear hierarchy and practices relaxation techniques. The goal is for the client to reach the most feared object or action and be able to react with calmness and control.

Symptoms of Burnout

At times, counselors may experience a sense of disinterest or disengagement from their work, which may signal burnout. Symptoms of burnout can include physical symptoms, such as fatigue, headaches, insomnia, and decreased resistance to illness. Emotional symptoms can include depression, anxiety, boredom, lack of empathy, cynicism, and anger. Burnout may be a result of overworking and/or providing service to clients who are not progressing in therapy, thus causing counselors to feel incompetent and ineffective. It is important to know the warning signs of burnout and engage in self-care, which may involve taking a vacation; getting increased supervision or therapy; making changes to one's hours, fees, or practice; or seeking continuing education options.

Warning Signs to Consider Before Expressing Personal Feelings

In rare cases, it may be appropriate for counselors to self-disclose to clients. It is important to remember that the therapeutic process is to help clients, not indirectly benefit counselors. First and foremost, counselors should consider the intent and who will benefit from their self-disclosure. It is not appropriate for clients to be burdened with counselors' emotions, as it could shift the atmosphere and power dynamic of therapy. Counselors can disclose an emotional reaction to content from clients, provided it is for the benefit of the clients. Counselors should be cognizant of their clients' level of functioning and issues prior to any purposeful self-disclosure to ensure professional boundaries are maintained.

Support System

As part of the intake process and initial sessions, counselors need to explore and understand clients' existing support systems. All individuals have varying degrees of social support, which can include friends, family, and community. Counselors can help clients evaluate their level of support and determine how the support system can help during counseling and after it has ended. It may be necessary to help clients find ways to develop additional support, such as through groups or organizations. A support system is necessary to provide help, encouragement, and care.

Characteristics of Willingness to Change

Entering into counseling can provoke anxiety, fear, and resistance to change. Clients may have both internal and external reasons to want or need to change but exhibit some unwillingness to do so. Clients with internal or intrinsic motivation understand that they need to change to move forward, grow, and achieve personal goals. External factors, such as mandated counseling, can be motivating, but may create additional resistance. Clients will be more motivated and willing to change when they have a vested interest in the process and believe they will achieve a successful outcome. Commitment to the process is essential, especially considering that counseling may not seem enjoyable or even interesting but may be necessary.

Group Work

Individuals seeking counseling may benefit from group work in addition to, or in place of, individual counseling. Groups focus on nonpathological issues, such as personal, physical/medical, social, or vocational, and act to support and encourage growth. Groups are popular for addictions, eating disorders or weight loss, grief, anxiety, and parenting. They can be homogenous and share demographic information and goals or can be heterogeneous and diverse with multifaceted goals. Group members

benefit from the process through sharing and the ability to learn new ways to react and cope with difficulties. It is essential that groups have a trained leader to help create structure, boundaries, and rules and keep the group on track.

Spirituality

Spirituality is a component of overall wellness and can be incorporated into the counseling process. It must be noted that spirituality is different from religion, although individuals may define the concepts in different ways. A client's spiritual views may encompass his or her higher sense of purpose, meaning, the reason for existence, worldview, and sense of place in the universe. Counselors need to be aware of their own spirituality and be able to appropriately support a client without imposing or rejecting their spiritual views. Spiritual practices that can be helpful in counseling include meditation, prayer, mindfulness, and reflection.

Maslow's Hierarchy of Needs

Abraham Maslow believed that all humans have basic needs, that, once filled, allow movement onto higher-level functioning. The hierarchy is depicted as a pyramid with biological and psychological needs at the base. The base level includes the need for food, shelter, warmth, air, sex, and sleep. The next level, safety, is the need for personal security, stability, laws, and social order. The third level reflects the need for love and a sense of belonging, which can include both personal and professional relationships. The fourth level is esteem needs and was updated to include cognitive and aesthetic needs. These include the need for self-esteem, status, prestige, knowledge, and an appreciation for beauty and balance. The top level of the pyramid is self-actualization when an individual has reached his or her potential, is fulfilled, and finds meaning in life. It can also include the process of helping others achieve self-actualization. It's important to realize that if clients are not having their very basic needs met (food, shelter, etc.), they will have great difficulty working on higher goals that contribute to their mental and emotional well-being.

Wellness

The concept of wellness is multidimensional and includes six aspects of health: occupational, physical, emotional, spiritual, intellectual, and social. Wellness is holistic and stresses the need for individuals to find balance and maximize their potential. It can be considered to be more of a luxury than an essential need. Wellness is a higher level of functioning for those who have their basic needs met and are seeking a more successful existence.

Finding Happiness

Happiness can be defined in many ways, and individuals may have challenges in arriving at a state where they feel entirely happy. Research on happiness shows that it is small things, like activities, and not hypothetical future events or material possessions that create the most happiness. Counseling can assist in helping individuals explore times when they felt happy and work on ways to increase and maintain their happiness. By asking clients about past happy times and what about those times made them feel happy, the counselor will be able to help clients explore how to feel happier in the present. It is important to recognize that future achievements may not produce desired happiness, such as "I will be happy when …". Rather, counselors should focus on helping clients appreciate what makes them happy in the present moment and how to use that happiness to feel more fulfilled each day.

Structured and Unstructured Helping Relationships

Individuals can get help and support from many types of relationships, both structured and unstructured. Structured relationships include those with professional helpers, such as counselors, therapists, medical professionals, and social workers. These relationships have clear goals and are time-limited both in session and overall duration. Unstructured relationships also provide support but are more ambiguous and ongoing. These can include community support, groups, friends, family, and activities such as workshops or retreats.

Models of a Helper

Gerard Egan developed a model for helping outlined in his book, *The Skilled Helper*. Egan drew from several theorists, including Rogers, Carkhuff, and Albert Bandura, to create a three-stage model for helping. The phases of the model are identifying the present situation or scenario, defining the desired scenario, and developing a strategy to achieve it. The model provides a framework and map that clients can internalize for use when faced with a problem. It was designed to empower individuals to develop skills and confidence to solve problems outside of a helping relationship.

Congruence

The term *congruence* is associated with the person-centered work of Carl Rogers. Congruence can be defined as genuineness on the part of counselors, in that there is agreement on their words and actions. Counselors display congruence when their body language, affect, and words correspond to demonstrate genuine concern for the client. Lack of congruence is revealed when counselors express concern but at the same time seem bored, disinterested, or use language that does not indicate a true understanding of the client. Counselors who are nonreactive or act as a blank screen for clients are not expressing congruence. Rogers considered congruence to be essential for effective counseling.

Touch

There is some controversy over the use of touch in counseling. Studies have found that touch, such as a pat on the shoulder or a hug, can be very beneficial to some clients. Touch can provide comfort, reassurance, grounding, and support. However, there is an argument that touch violates personal boundaries and can be considered unethical. Touch is also interpreted in widely different ways across cultures; the United States is considered a "low touch" culture. For counselors, it is important to understand ethical and intercultural issues surrounding the use of touch and to use it only if and when it is needed and can be therapeutically beneficial.

Imagery

Guided imagery can be a powerful tool in the counseling process. Guided imagery, which draws upon the mind-body connection, can be used to help the client alleviate anxiety, relax, and control or change negative thoughts or feelings. A counselor, who helps the client envision a place of relaxation and calm, guides the process. The counselor encourages the client to visualize and relax into the details of the image. Clients can also envision the successful outcome of a situation or imagine themselves handling a stressful situation. Once learned, clients can practice imagery on their own to help reduce stress and anxiety.

External Stress, Internal Distress, and Transitional Stress

Crisis situations and stress have a variety of causes. External stress exists outside of a person's control and can include natural disasters, loss, illness of self or a family member, crime, poverty, or job change. Internal distress is the reaction to external stress but may be chronic and exist at all times due to an individual's coping skills and personal choices. Positive events, such as marriage, childbirth, a new job, or relocation, can cause eustress, which is considered positive stress. Major life changes can cause transitional stress, which may be short term but still requires strategies for managing. Stress management techniques include maintaining one's physical health, adequate sleep, relaxation techniques, and engaging in enjoyable activities or hobbies.

Practice Questions

1. Symptoms of professional burnout consist of fatigue, headache, insomnia, depression, anxiety, or boredom, among others. When does burnout in counselors and helping professionals occur?
    a. When countertransference is not managed
    b. When counselors become desensitized to client issues
    c. When counselors are overworked
    d. When clients regularly cancel or don't show

2. Robert Carkhuff wrote *Toward Effective Counseling and Psychotherapy*, a book wherein he discovered that therapeutic interventions did not always have a long-term positive impact on clients. Carkhuff also created a five-point empathy scale, designed to measure what?
    a. Counselor's ability to accurately reflect
    b. Effectiveness of counselor
    c. Defensiveness of counselor
    d. Adequate structuring of sessions

3. Reflection is a practice where counselors acknowledge the meaning behind a client's words. Why do counselors use reflection in sessions?
    a. To help clients understand underlying emotions
    b. To provide advice
    c. To set goals for sessions
    d. To allow for silence

4. Carl Rogers believed three core conditions must exist for effective counseling. What are those conditions?
    a. Trust, empathy, and kindness
    b. Empathy, positive regard, and kindness
    c. Genuineness, trust, and congruence
    d. Empathy, positive regard, and congruence

5. Positive interactions help develop the therapeutic relationship and encourage clients to meet their goals. What are the four stages of a positive interaction in counseling?
    a. Exploration, consolidation, planning, and termination
    b. Initiation, clarification, structure, and relationship
    c. Initiation, consolidation, planning, and termination
    d. Exploration, clarification, planning, and relationship

6. Relationship building is the beginning process of the client-counselor relationship. What are the phases of relationship building?
    a. Introduction, goal setting, resistance, and change
    b. Initiation, clarification, structure, and relationship
    c. Exploration, clarification, planning, and termination
    d. Clarification, consolidation, structure, and relationship

7. When does negative transference occur?
   a. When counselors project feelings onto clients
   b. When clients project feelings toward another person in the past onto the counselor
   c. When multiple roles exist between a therapist and a client
   d. When clients become angry or hostile toward counselors

8. What are the differences between substantive advice and process advice?
   a. Substantive is nondirective; process is directive.
   b. Substantive is directive; process is encouraging.
   c. Substantive is directive; process is empowering.
   d. Substantive is fact-based; process is feeling-based.

9. What are the four phases of a crisis as defined by Gerald Caplan?
   a. Threat, escalation, resolution, follow-up
   b. Threat, intervention, climax, resolution
   c. Threat, rapport, strategy, treatment
   d. Threat, escalation, acute crisis, climax

10. Albert Roberts designed a seven-stage model to deal with a crisis and provide effective intervention and support. What are the initial three tasks of Roberts's seven-stage model of crisis intervention?
   a. Assessments, identifying problems, and referring out
   b. Establishing contact, providing counseling, and referring out
   c. Assessments, establishing rapport, and identifying cause of crisis
   d. Intervention, assessments, and treatment

11. Critical Incident Stress Debriefing (CISD) is short-term work done in small groups and is not considered psychotherapy. Techniques used include processing, defusing, ventilating, and validating thoughts, experiences, feeling and emotions. CISD is designed for which of the following?
   a. Primary trauma victims
   b. Human resources professionals
   c. First responders
   d. Secondary trauma victims

12. When is Critical Incident Stress Debriefing (CISD) most effective?
   a. When it is provided to individuals
   b. When it is provided by trained mental health professionals
   c. When it is provided within seven days of the incident
   d. When it is provided within 24 to 72 hours

13. What are the stages for Kubler-Ross' five-stage model for grief?
   a. Anger, denial, bargaining, resolution, sadness
   b. Denial, anger, bargaining, depression, acceptance
   c. Denial, panic, sadness, anger, frustration
   d. Sadness, anger, bargaining, denial, acceptance

14. How does instrumental grieving differ from intuitive grieving?
   a. Instrumental is thinking; intuitive is feeling.
   b. Instrumental is action-oriented; intuitive is passive.
   c. Instrumental is more feminine; intuitive is more masculine.
   d. Instrumental is anger; intuitive is acceptance.

15. Counselors may feel there are certain situations where it becomes necessary to make referrals for clients to seek other counselors, also known as "referring out." Which of the following is NOT a reason for counselors to refer out?
   a. Client issues outside of the counselor scope of practice
   b. Dislike for client
   c. Client need for specialized service
   d. Counselor retiring or taking leave from practice

16. What are SMART goals?
   a. Specific, meaningful, achievable, realistic, and time-sensitive
   b. Special, manageable, action-oriented, realistic, and timely
   c. Specific, measurable, action-oriented, relevant, and time-bound
   d. Specific, measurable, achievable, relevant, and time-bound

17. How does negative reinforcement encourage specific behaviors?
   a. Removing unwanted stimuli
   b. Adding desired stimuli
   c. Punishing clients for unwanted behavior
   d. Extinction of stimuli

18. Desensitization is a behavior modification technique designed to replace an anxiety-producing stimulus with a relaxation response. Which is NOT one of the stages of desensitization?
   a. Exposure to the object or action of fear
   b. Avoidance of the object or action of fear
   c. Creation of a fear hierarchy
   d. Learning relaxation techniques

19. When does modeling occur in the counseling process?
   a. When counselors model clients' feelings back to them
   b. When clients provide counselors with an ideal image of themselves to achieve
   c. When clients are told how to behave by counselors
   d. When counselors demonstrate appropriate reactions and behaviors for clients to follow

20. Maslow's hierarchy of needs is composed of five levels. Which needs are included in Level 4?
   a. Cognitive and aesthetic
   b. Food and shelter
   c. Safety and order
   d. Love and belonging

Answer Explanations

1. C: Although challenges with clients (Choices *A, B,* and *D*) can contribute to counselor burnout, the main reasons for burnout are overwork and lack of appropriate supervision.

2. B: Effectiveness of counselor. Carkhuff's scale measured the degree to which a counselor was providing empathy, genuineness, concreteness, and respect. The scale measures effectiveness but refers to how defensive a counselor is toward the client. Choice *A*, accurate reflection, is a counseling skill, but not one measured by Carkhuff. Defensiveness of counselor is incorrect, Choice *C*. Choice *D*, structuring of sessions, is important, but it is not the correct answer.

3. A: To help clients understand underlying emotions. Reflection is also referred to as "reflection of feeling" and is used for counselors to indicate that they both hear and understand the meanings and emotions behind a client's words. Counselors do not provide advice during reflection, but let the client know they are being heard, so Choice *B* is incorrect. There is also no goal setting during this time, because it's important for the client to know their emotions are being validated, making Choice *C* incorrect. When reflection happens, the counselor provides communication to the client, so silence has less to do with it than Choice *A*, making Choice *D* incorrect.

4. D: Carl Rogers developed the person-centered approach to counseling, which stressed the important of the counseling relationship, as well as the need to evaluate therapy for effectiveness. Carl Rogers's three core conditions for effective counseling were empathy, positive regard, and congruence (genuineness).

5. A: The stages of positive interaction are exploration, consolidation, planning, and termination.

> Stage 1. Exploration of feelings and definition of problem: The counselor will use rapport-building skills, define the structure of the counseling process and relationship, and work with the client on goal setting.

> Stage 2. Consolidation: The client integrates the information and guidance from the counselor, allowing him or her to gain additional coping skills and identify alternate ways to solve problems.

> Stage 3. Planning: The client begins employing techniques learned in counseling and prepares to manage on his or her own.

> Stage 4. Termination: This is the ending of the therapeutic relationship, when the client feels equipped to manage problems independently and has fully integrated techniques learned in counseling.

6. B: The phases for relationship building are initiation, clarification, structure, and relationship:

> Phase 1. Initiation, or entry phase: This is the introduction to the counseling process, which sets the stage for the development of the client/counselor relationship.

> Phase 2. Clarification phase: This phase defines the problem and need for the therapeutic relationship.

Phase 3. Structure phase: The counselor defines the specifics of the relationship, its intended outcomes, and the responsibilities of both parties.

Phase 4. Relationship phase: The client and counselor have developed a relationship and will work toward mutually agreed-upon goals.

7. D: Negative transference can result in clients becoming angry and hostile toward the counselor. Although transference is an essential part of psychoanalytic counseling, negative transference can be difficult to manage and must be dealt with in order for therapy to progress. Choice *A*, when counselors project feelings onto clients, is called countertransference. Choice *B*, when clients project feelings toward another person in the past onto the counselor, is known as transference. Choice *C*, when multiple roles exist between a counselor and client, is known as a dual relationship.

8. C: Substantive advice can be considered directive and may involve the counselor imposing his or her opinions onto clients. Process advice is more empowering and helps clients navigate options for solving their own issues. In some situations, it may be appropriate for the counselor to offer process advice; it is less likely that substantive advice should be given.

9. D: Caplan's phases are threat, escalation, acute crisis, climax:

- Initial threat or event, which triggers a response. The individual may be able to employ coping skills or defense mechanisms to avoid a crisis.

- Escalation, during which initial attempts to manage the crisis are ineffective and the individual begins to experience increased distress.

- Acute crisis phase, during which anxiety continues and may intensify to panic or a fight-or-flight response. There are still attempts to problem-solve during this phase, and new tactics may be used.

- Climax of the crisis when solutions have failed; the individual may experience personality disorganization and become severely depressed, violent, and possibly suicidal.

10. C: Assessments, establishing rapport, and identifying cause of crisis. Briefly, Roberts's seven phases of crisis management are:

- Biopsychosocial assessments
- Making contact and quickly establishing rapport
- Identifying problems and possible cause of crisis
- Providing counseling
- Working on coping strategies
- Implementing an action plan for treatment
- Follow-up

11. D: Critical Incident Stress Debriefing (CISD) is best suited to secondary trauma victims. First-degree victims need more direct assistance, making Choice *A* incorrect. HR professionals and first responders can provide needed help, making Choices *B* and *C* incorrect.

12. D: Critical Incident Stress Debriefing (CISD) is most effective when offered within 24 to 72 hours of an event. It can be provided by any trained individual, including HR or mental health professionals, and is intended for groups of secondary trauma victims.

13. B: Denial, anger, bargaining, depression, and acceptance are the five stages of grief according to Kubler-Ross. Sadness, frustration, and resolution are not part of her stages, making Choices *A*, *C*, and *D* incorrect.

14. A: There is thought to be two types of grieving: instrumental grieving and intuitive grieving. Instrumental is more thinking-based and about solving problems rather than feeling, and is viewed as a more masculine approach to grief. Intuitive is more emotional and about sharing and processing feelings, and is considered a more feminine approach to grief.

15. B: Counselors should refrain from referring out due to dislike for a client. This risks a client feeling abandoned and may be considered unethical. Needs of the client should be placed before those of the counselor. Counselors can refer out when retiring, taking a leave, when a client is out of the scope of their practice or expertise, or when a client needs specialized care, making Choices *A*, *C*, and *D* incorrect.

16. D: SMART goals are a way of planning an effective goal-setting and goal-accomplishing process. The SMART goals are specific, measurable, achievable, relevant, and time-bound. Specific is being detailed about what the goal is and how it can be accomplished. Measurable is tracking the goal or improvements to keep up motivation, achievable is making sure the goal is realistic, relevant is asking yourself if it's the right time for the goal, or if you're the right person for it, and time-bound is setting a clear date to achieve the goal by so as not to lose focus. Choices *A*, *B*, and *C* are incorrect.

17. A: Negative reinforcement encourages specific behaviors by removing unwanted stimuli. An example of this is putting on a seat belt to remove the sound of the car dinging (reminding you to fasten your seat belt). Choice *B*, adding desired stimuli, is considered positive reinforcement. Negative reinforcement does not include punishment for unwanted behavior, which makes Choice *C* incorrect. Negative reinforcement also does not include extinction of stimuli (Choice *D*), but the removal of unwanted stimuli; the "unwanted" here is important.

18. B: Avoidance of the object or action of fear is NOT one of the stages of desensitization. Exposure to the object, creating a fear hierarchy, and learning relaxation techniques while being exposed are stages of systematic desensitization.

19. D: Modeling occurs in the counseling process when counselors demonstrate (or model) appropriate reactions and behaviors for clients to follow. Modeling is nonverbal and helps clients learn appropriate behavior through observation.

20. A: Maslow's hierarchy of needs is composed of five levels. The fourth level is esteem needs and was updated to include cognitive and aesthetic needs. This includes the need for self-esteem, status, prestige, knowledge, and an appreciation for beauty and balance. Level 1 is the need for food, shelter, warmth, air, sex, and sleep. Level 2 is the need for safety, personal security, stability, laws, and social order. Level 3 reflects the need for love and a sense of belonging. Level 5 of the pyramid is self-actualization.

Group Counseling and Group Work

Classification of Groups Designed by Gerald Caplan

Gerald Caplan, most well known for his crisis intervention theories, defined three levels of groups. Primary groups focus on healthy living and coping strategies. These groups, also referred to as support, guidance, or psychoeducational, may help prevent unwanted consequences by teaching healthier alternatives. Secondary groups deal more with existing problems and work to reduce or prevent their severity. Also referred to as counseling groups, the focus is on short-term concerns. Tertiary groups are designed for individuals with more serious pathology and include members who are likely receiving individual psychotherapy in addition to the group.

Group Dynamics and Cohesion

Broadly speaking, anything that impacts the group can be considered dynamic. The word *dynamic* means change, activity, or progress. Thus, a group is constantly adapting and evolving. Dynamics are the interrelationships between the members, which include the leadership style, decision-making, and cohesiveness. Cohesiveness is the degree to which the group sticks together. There are two types of cohesion: task and social. Task is the level at which the group works to achieve a common objective. Social cohesiveness refers to the interpersonal relationships within the group.

Types of Groups and Primary Goals

- Guidance/psychoeducational: This type of group is designed to teach or guide individuals to develop or maintain specific skills. This group is used to help prevent problems (such as substance abuse or teen pregnancy) and teach alternative options, problem solving, and coping skills. They are considered structured groups, as there are defined tasks and goals.

- Counseling: This type of group provides additional support to members experiencing stress but not major psychological issues.

- Psychotherapy: This type of group provides a therapeutic intervention for members experiencing more acute issues and must be led by a trained counselor or psychotherapist.

- Self-help: This is a more informal group that does not have a designated leader. Alcoholics Anonymous is a self-help group.

- T-group: This is an experiential or training group designed to help individuals facilitate change.

- Task: This group is formed to complete a specific task or goal. These can include committees, focus groups, or work groups.

- Psychoanalytic: These groups are based on Freudian theories and used to gain conscious awareness of unconscious conflicts. These groups can be intense and long term but are designed to facilitate major insights and change.

- Cognitive behavioral: This is a task-focused group to help individuals understand how thoughts impact behaviors and develop more functional patterns.

Leadership Styles

There are three main styles of leading groups:

- Autocratic: This leader is authoritarian and sets clear rules, boundaries, and goals for the group. This type can be beneficial in situations where there are time or resource limitations, constant changes to membership, or the need to coordinate with other groups. This type of leadership can create resentment and dissatisfaction, as it is unilateral and strict.

- Democratic: This leader is considered the fairest by taking into consideration ideas and choices of the group. Not to be confused with the political usage, these leaders do not wield specific power or prestige; rather, they work to maintain a participatory style and harmonious atmosphere.

- Laissez-Faire: This is the most relaxed style of leadership; group members are responsible for all aspects of decision-making. Laissez-faire is an absence of leadership, which works best with motivated, self-directed members.

Roles of Group Members

Members serve different roles in the group and can change their roles as the group progresses. There are both functional and nonfunctional roles. Functional roles assist the group and include the energizer, harmonizer, tension reliever, and gatekeeper. Nonfunctional roles can disrupt and hinder the group and include the interrogator, dominator, monopolizer, aggressor, and recognition seeker. Other roles include victim, scapegoat, and follower, who are not overtly negative but do not assist in positive group functioning.

Core Skills Needed by Group Counselors

Group counselors need strong interpersonal and management skills to effectively supervise groups. Specific skills needed include:

- Use of counseling and therapeutic techniques, such as reflection, empathy, genuineness, positive regard, and restatement
- Understanding group counseling dynamics in theory and practice
- Ability to facilitate discussions by starting and ending sessions and keeping the group on track
- Blocking actions of members disrupting the group
- Moderating discussions and asking appropriate questions
- Being able to encourage and support the group as a whole and as individuals
- Ensuring members are working toward their goals and the goals of the group
- Comfort with confrontation and the ability to manage differing personalities and needs
- Summarizing sessions and goal setting
- Modeling appropriate behavior
- Nondefensiveness
- Understanding of cultural differences that impact individuals and respecting diversity
- Encouraging participation while understanding individual needs
- Stamina and sense of humor

Positive Aspects of Working with a Co-Leader

Co-leadership is widely used in group therapy sessions and is found to have many beneficial aspects. Co-leadership may be used as a way to train therapists to lead groups and is found to have positive impacts, especially in larger groups. Having two leaders can help ensure that all members get attention, can actively participate, and assist the group in accomplishing more. Co-leadership can be detrimental if leaders do not get along or cannot form a cooperative and united management team for the group.

Stages of a Group

Several theories outline the developmental stages of a group. One of the most well-known is Bruce Tuckman's four-stage model: forming, storming, norming, and performing. Forming is the stage where the group members are just beginning to get acquainted and may be anxious and less vocal. Storming involves conflict, discord, and struggles to agree upon a leader. Norming is the agreement stage, during which a leader is chosen and conflicts begin to resolve. Performing is the point at which the group becomes effective at achieving defined tasks. A fifth stage, Adjourning, was added, which defines the point at which the group terminates. Other group development theories include that of Irvin D. Yalom, whose three-stage model included orientation, conflict/dominance, and development of cohesiveness. Gerald Corey's stages included initia l, transition, working, and termination. All three theories share similar progressions of the group process.

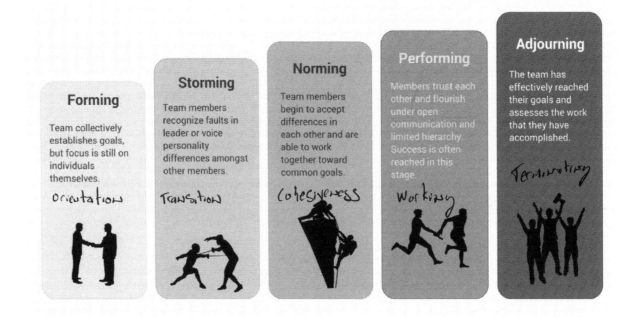

Purpose of Family Counseling

Just as individuals need help and support, family units need guidance in dealing with problems, coping with stressors, and learning ways to function more effectively. The goals of family counseling are to identify and change dysfunctional patterns, increase communication, and use the power of relationships to heal and stabilize the family unit. Family counseling can include nuclear families, extended families, and anyone who has an impact on the familial relationship. Family counseling helps to build love and support, thus creating stronger and healthier families.

Psychoanalytic Theory and Group Work

Based on Freudian theories, psychoanalytic groups are intensive and long-term forms of group therapy. These groups focus on early childhood relationships, unconscious processes, and the resolution of past relationship conflicts. Group members may use each other and the group leader to re-experience past relationships and work to develop insight and self-awareness. Transference and countertransference are essential processes in psychoanalytic groups, and the leader's role is to facilitate analysis, interpretation, and resolution of individual and group dynamics.

Gestalt Theory and Group Work

Based on the work of Fritz Perls, Gestalt group work began as an alternative to the more intense psychoanalytic group process. Gestalt, from the German word for *shape* or *form*, encourages increased emotional awareness, freedom, and self-direction. It is a holistic model that helps clients focus on the present and work toward personal growth and balance. Specific techniques used are experimental exercises, such as the empty chair technique, where a client uses an empty chair to resolve feelings toward a specific person or sits in the chair to act as that person.

Person-Centered Theory and Group Work

Applying the Rogerian principles of genuineness, positive regard, and empathy, person-centered group work is designed to help individuals increase self-awareness, self-acceptance, and openness and decrease defensiveness. The group leader is nondirective and may act as more of a member than an expert. Person-centered groups may progress more organically, as there is less structure and more focus on listening and reflection.

Behavioral Counseling Groups

Behavioral groups are more structured and designed to help extinguish unwanted behaviors or increase more functional thoughts and actions. Behavior modification techniques such as reinforcement, modeling, extinction, and desensitization are used. The leader of a behavioral group is an expert and directive and sets a clear agenda. These groups focus less on emotional content and processing and more on increasing levels of functioning through behavior modification.

Transactional Analysis Theory and Group Work

Through the study of psychoanalysis and human interaction, Eric Berne developed transactional analysis, which is easily applied to group settings. The focus of the work is on human interactions and helping individuals develop autonomy by learning awareness, spontaneity, and the capacity for intimacy. Group members support each other through positive interactions that help empower them to make better decisions. Group leaders have three main functions: protection, permission, and potency. These involve keeping members safe, providing directives, and using appropriate counseling interventions. Examples of these functions would be protecting by communication the message that the group and counselor will be there when the client is scared or worried, and the group and therapist give the client permission to do whatever he or she was previously told wasn't allowed (such as communicating feelings or asking for what he or she needs). Finally, the degree to which the client is protecting or giving permission to him or herself will affect the therapeutic potency (or how much the mind, internal self-talk, and emotions are affected).

Reality Theory and Group Work

Reality theory focuses on the present; the goal is for members to understand consequences of decisions and learn to get their basic needs met. Basic needs include survival, love, belonging, power, freedom, and fun. Once their needs are met, members can focus on controlling their behavior. The leader's role is to instill trust in the members, help them provide each other feedback, and teach them to apply what is learned in therapy to their life.

Rational Emotive Behavior Counseling Groups

Rational Emotive (REBT) counseling is based on the cognitive behavioral theories of Albert Ellis. REBT focuses on the present, with the goal of improving cognitive, emotional, and behavior functioning. Clients are taught to focus on adaptive behaviors rather than dwell on past events. Group leaders in REBT are directive and act as both therapists and educators. Their role is to help members identify faulty thought patterns and challenge their irrational beliefs. Ellis defined the main goals as gaining acceptance of self and others and dropping inflexible and maladaptive thoughts and behaviors.

Structured vs. Unstructured Group Sessions

Structured exercises are important, especially at the start of a new group, to help members open up and gain trust with one another. Research has shown that too much structure can be detrimental for a group and causes overreliance on the leader. Yalom found that excessive structure could also cause the group to skip over necessary stages of development. It was also found that leaders of highly structured groups were more popular with the members; however, the group overall was less effective.

Adlerian Theory and Group Work

Alfred Adler was one of the first psychologists to use group counseling, as he believed that individuals needed social structure to facilitate change. He found issues resulted from a lack of social connections, which could be addressed through a therapy group. Adlerian group therapy has four main goals: first, establishing and maintaining relationships with group members; second, understanding each individual's functioning based on his or her social and family experiences; third, gaining awareness and insight from interactions with, and feedback from, group members; and fourth, bringing change into action through reorientation to society with improved self-esteem. Adlerian group leaders act as guides and role models and are actively involved with the group.

Important Terms

Blocking: the act of the group leader stopping unwanted behaviors from members that may be harmful or hurtful or violate confidentiality

Closed Group: a group that, once formed, does not accept new members; may be more cohesive and stable than an open group

Group Norms: the do's and don'ts and expected behaviors of a group; may be verbalized or implied

Group Work Grid: R.K. Coyne's theory on four levels of intervention: individual, interpersonal, organization, and community

Horizontal Interventions: strategy in which the leader interacts with the group as a whole; also known as *interpersonal*

Stephen Karpman's Drama Triangle: a term from transactional analysis used to identify roles of persecutor, rescuer, and victim in relationships

Linking: group leader relating members' stories or situations to enhance interaction and cohesion

Open Group: group with ever-changing membership

Risky Shift Phenomenon: group decisions that are less conservative (riskier) as a result of group discussions

Self-Help Group: support group with common issues and goals; most often voluntary and without professional leaders, these groups share and learn from each other

Sociometry: the measurement of social relationships developed by Jacob Moreno

Task Roles: can include helpful roles, such as task and maintenance, and unhelpful roles, such as individual/self-serving

T-group: training (may also be referred to as *sensitivity* or *encounter*) groups that focus on relationships in business settings

Vertical Intervention: strategy in which the leader focuses on individual group members; also known as *intrapersonal*

Practice Questions

1. Which type of psychological group deals with long-standing pathology?
    a. Tertiary
    b. Secondary
    c. Primary
    d. Psychoeducational

2. Dynamics deal with the interrelationships between the members, which include the leadership style, decision-making, and cohesiveness. Which of the following defines the dynamics of a group?
    a. Positive leadership
    b. Anything that impacts the group
    c. Lack of cohesiveness
    d. Norming

3. One of the three main styles of leadership for managing a group is an autocratic leadership. What are autocratic leaders most likely to lead with?
    a. Consensus and belonging
    b. Little to no structure
    c. Empathy and goal setting
    d. Control and power

4. What are groups called that provide guidance, problem prevention, and skills building?
    a. Psychoeducational
    b. Structured
    c. Gestalt
    d. Psychodynamic

5. Group counselors need strong interpersonal skills in order to lead groups. Which skill is NOT required for a group counselor?
    a. Encouragement
    b. Support
    c. Confrontation
    d. Crisis intervention training

6. What do Yalom's stages of group development include?
    a. Forming, norming, storming, and performing
    b. Orientation, storming, working, and adjourning
    c. Orientation, conflict/dominance, and development of cohesiveness
    d. Initial, transition, working, and termination

7. The storming phase of group development refers to which activities?
    a. Anxiety from some members of the group and difficulty opening up
    b. Group termination and moving on
    c. Use of role-playing
    d. Vying for leadership and group conflict

8. Family units need guidance just as individuals do in dealing with problems and learning how to function more effectively. Which is NOT a goal of family therapy?
    a. Resolving intrapsychic conflicts
    b. Increasing effective communication
    c. Creating more effective patterns
    d. Improving overall functioning and stability

9. Which of the following is a holistic model that helps clients focus on the present and work toward personal growth and balance?
    a. Gestalt
    b. Person-centered
    c. Rational Emotive
    d. Jungian

10. Psychoanalytic groups focus on what specific solution?
    a. Decreasing anxiety
    b. Resolution of childhood issues
    c. Resolution of current relationship issues
    d. Increasing daily functioning

11. The empty chair technique is used by what type of group therapy and for what reason?
    a. Person-centered, to put oneself in another's situation and build empathy
    b. Gestalt, to resolve emotional issues with another person
    c. Psychoanalytic, to resolve issues with parents or authority figures
    d. Transactional analysis, to understand and edit life scripts

12. Blocking refers to what type of act in group counseling?
    a. Leader putting a stop to negative behavior
    b. Members being disruptive to process
    c. Leader locking the door to prevent members from exiting
    d. Existing members not welcoming new members to group

13. Risky shift phenomenon refers to what aspects of group dynamics?
    a. Groups becoming increasingly risk-averse
    b. Groups become less risk-averse
    c. Leaders encouraging individual members to take risks
    d. Closed groups considering taking on new members

14. Vertical interventions occur when the group leader focuses on which of the following?
    a. Individuals rather than the group
    b. The group rather than individuals
    c. Both the individuals and the larger group
    d. Group dynamics

15. Which of the following is another term for horizontal interventions in group counseling?
    a. Interpersonal
    b. Intrapersonal
    c. Individual
    d. Organizational

Answer Explanations

1. A: Tertiary groups deal with long-standing pathology; think of it as the third and most acute level. Tertiary groups are used to facilitate long-term personality change or rehabilitation. Primary groups are educational in nature, making Choice *C* incorrect. Secondary groups are focused on counseling, making Choice *B* incorrect. Psychoeducational group structure refers to a type of group designed to teach individuals to develop or maintain specific skills, making Choice *D* incorrect.

2. B: The word *dynamic* means activity, change, or progress; thus, dynamics are anything that affect (or change) the group. Group dynamics refers to any interactions and processes of the group. Choice *A*, positive leadership, can be part of a leadership style of a group, but it does not define group dynamics. Choice *C*, lack of cohesiveness, is the inability to form a united whole, and is incorrect. Choice *D*, norming, is one of the stages of group development and involves the time where the group becomes a cohesive unit.

3. D: Autocratic leaders are most likely to lead with control and power. Democratic leaders use consensus and belonging, making Choice *A* incorrect. Laissez-faire leaders operate with little to no structure, making Choice *B* incorrect. Choice *C* is not a group of characteristics for any main style of leadership.

4. A: Groups that provide guidance, problem prevention, and skills building are psychoeducational and may also be called guidance groups. Structured groups, Choice *B*, refer to how the group is set up—whether it is rigid in how it operates or more fluid. Gestalt groups, Choice *C*, are an alternative to intense psychoanalytic groups. Group members work on emotional awareness, freedom, and self-direction. Psychodynamic groups, Choice *D*, are long-term therapeutic groups made up of individuals who all have similar mental health diagnoses.

5. D: Crisis intervention training is not needed for a group counselor, but the ability to encourage, support, and confront are necessary skills. A group counselor needs to have all the skills and training that an individual counselor would require. Encouraging group members, being supportive, and the ability to confront behavior are all skills needed and utilized by counselors.

6. C: Yalom's three-stage model included orientation, conflict/dominance, and development of cohesiveness. Corey's stages included initial, transition, working, and termination, making Choice *D* incorrect. Forming, norming, storming, and performing are included in Tuckman's theory, making Choice *A* incorrect. Choice *B* is a mixture of all of these stages.

7. D: Storming is the vying for leadership and conflict in the group. Storming involves conflict, discord, and struggles to agree upon a leader. Choice *A* refers to the forming phase. Forming is the stage where the group members are just beginning to get acquainted and may be anxious and less vocal. Choice *B* is adjourning, which is the point in which the group is terminated. Role-play is not relevant to group development but is a technique used in therapy to help clients work through how they would handle conflict with individuals.

8. A: Choices *B*, *C*, and *D* are all goals of family therapy. Resolving intrapsychic conflicts is a function associated with psychoanalysis and not family therapy.

9. A: Gestalt is a holistic model that helps clients focus on the present and work toward personal growth and balance. Person-centered, Choice *B*, is a group method designed to help members increase self-awareness, self-acceptance, and openness, and decrease defensiveness. These groups have less structure and focus on listening and reflecting. Rational Emotive group therapy, Choice *C*, is based on cognitive behavioral theories. The focus is on the present with the goal of improving cognitive, emotional, and behavior functioning. Group members focus on adaptive behaviors. Jungian, Choice *D*, is a form of therapy but not a specific group therapy. In Jungian therapy, the therapist is an analyst who works with the client to merge the unconscious parts of the psyche with the conscious parts of the self.

10. B: Resolving childhood issues is the crux of psychoanalytic therapy, in individuals or in groups. Decreasing anxiety, Choice *A*, can be a goal of individual therapy as well as Rational Emotive or psychodynamic groups. Resolution of current relationship issues, Choice *C*, is the goal of family therapy. Increasing daily functioning, Choice *D*, would be a goal of Rational Emotive as well as psychodynamic groups.

11. B: The empty chair technique is used in Gestalt to help resolve feelings toward another person. The other choices are merely the goals of those types of therapies. In person-centered therapy, Choice A, the goal of the counselor is to put himself or herself in another's situation and have empathy toward that person. One goal of psychoanalytic therapy, Choice *C*, is to resolve issues with parents or authority figures. Finally, in transactional analysis, Choice *D*, therapists work with clients to understand their life scripts and how they may be edited to have a more functional life.

12. A: Blocking refers to a group leader blocking or putting a stop to negative behavior of a group member. This can be harmful comments or anything that violates confidentiality or group norms. Members being disruptive to the process, Choice *B*, would be an example of conflict within the group. The leader locking the door to prevent exiting, Choice *C*, is not a technique used in group therapy. Existing members not welcoming new members, Choice *D*, could be an example of scapegoating a group member.

13. B: Risky shift phenomenon refers to groups becoming less risk-averse or riskier in their decisions. The act of sharing the risk among others makes individuals less conservative in their actions. Group leaders encouraging members to take more risks, Choice *C*, would fall under therapeutic techniques. Closed groups considering taking on new members, Choice *D*, would involve completely changing the type of group from closed to open.

14. A: Vertical interventions occur when the group leader focuses on individuals rather than the group (also referred to as *intrapersonal*). Choice *B* is incorrect; when the group leader focuses on the group as a whole rather than individuals, this is known as horizontal interventions, or interpersonal.

15. A: Horizontal interventions in group counseling are referred to as *interpersonal* and define when the leader works with the group as a whole rather than as individuals. Intrapersonal, Choice *B*, is another term for vertical interventions, which occurs when the group leader focuses on individuals rather than the group.

Career Counseling

History of Career Development

The vocational guidance movement began in the early 20th century. Social changes such as urbanization, the move away from agriculture, and the end of World War I made it necessary for individuals to take an active role in finding work. Changes in education, along with the growth of social work and psychometric testing, created the basis for vocational and career counseling. Two important figures whose practices became recognized theories were Jesse B. Davis and Frank Parsons.

Jesse B. Davis was an educator who developed early vocational guidance programs in public schools. Through these programs, he and other public school teachers used academic assignments to help students recognize and evaluate their career interests.

Another key figure in developing the field was Frank Parsons. A professor, lawyer, and educational reformer, Parsons is known as "the father of the vocational guidance movement." Because of his work and vocational modeling theories, the Vocational Bureau at Civic Service House was established in Boston, Massachusetts after his death in 1908. This entity later became affiliated with the Division of Education and the Graduate School of Business at Harvard University, where its function was to assist students with their transition from school to work. Parsons's theories were largely based on observations. Psychometric testing quantified some of his theories, but the later use of more scientific methods greatly helped to legitimize vocational counseling.

In 1913, the National Vocational Guidance Association was formed in Grand Rapids, Michigan. In 1985, this organization became the National Career Development Association (NCDA), which still exists today. The NCDA has thousands of members and is considered the first—and longest running—career development association.

Following World War II, Franklin Roosevelt's New Deal program helped returning veterans who were faced with injury, physical limitations, and unemployment. In 1944, the Servicemen's Readjustment Act (commonly known as the "G.I. Bill") was launched to provide higher education and employment options. Unfortunately, existing workers were also being displaced by returning veterans, which compounded the unemployment issues. These conditions created a greater need for professional services, including career counseling.

The final event to solidify career counseling as a profession was the 1957 launch of the Sputnik satellite by the former USSR (Union of Soviet Socialist Republics). In 1958, the U.S. responded by passing the National Defense Education Act (NDEA) to encourage the study of science. Funds from the NDEA were used to provide career interest testing, and also to hire and train school counselors. As a result, varying theories and approaches began to emerge.

Career Development Theories fall into the following general categories:

Trait Factor/Actuarial

The Trait Factor Theory is the one most closely associated with the work of Frank Parsons. Several theorists at the University of Minnesota (John Daley, Edmund G. Williamson, and Donald Paterson) developed theories on assessments and psychometrics, which were combined later with Parsons's vocational guidance principles. Originally referred to as "talent matching" or known as "personality x

environment fit," Parsons named it the Trait and Factor Theory of Occupational Choice. His approach focused on matching an individual's personal traits to occupations. Parson's theory had four essential components. First, he believed in individual traits: values, interests, skills, and personality characteristics. These traits could be combined in unique ways for each person, and could be recognized and classified. Second, there were factors (aspects and details) that made up each occupation. Third, by knowing an individual's unique set of traits (distinguishing qualities) and the requirements for any occupation, it was possible to identify a fit between a person and a career. Fourth, and finally, job satisfaction was at its highest when there was a strong correlation between the person (trait) and the occupation (factor). This theory was based on straightforward decision-making and the process of matching traits and factors. Broadly speaking, matching the person to the occupation, as explained above, is still widely used today as a form of career counseling.

Developmental Approach
In the 1950s, Eli Ginzberg created a career development model that illustrated this process as lifelong and evolving. This model was holistic in nature and allowed for the individual's career planning to be influenced by many factors, including their self-concept and life roles.

Decision Approach
H.B. Gelatt brought formal decision-making theories to career counseling. During the 1960s, he authored papers outlining the absence of theoretical framework for vocational counseling. His theory suggested that individuals choose an appropriate program of courses and a counselor facilitates in the decision-making process. The process should be systematic and predictive, with the student (or decision maker) assessing all probabilities and alternatives and then weighing the desirability of each possible outcome.

Psychological Approach
In the 1960s, John Holland developed theories that focused on personality types matching work environments. In his approach, individual personality types had the strongest impact on career decisions. The main themes were that individuals chose occupations based on their behavior. It was also noted that those with similar personalities tended to choose the same types of occupations. He also found that an individual's satisfaction with their employment depended on congruence between the job environment and their personality.

Constructivist Approach
The constructivist approach to career counseling focuses on the broader context of life planning and is a more philosophical approach to making career decisions. Individuals develop constructs about life, work, and themselves. While considering these constructs, individuals must find work that has meaning and adequately reflects their own reality, which is unique to their interpretations and life experiences.

Donald Super – Developmental Approach
Donald Super developed a framework for understanding career development as a constantly evolving process. He believed in many of Eli Ginzberg's theories and expanded on those ideas. He proposed broad stages of development that coincided with tasks, and substages that defined specific personal-growth milestones.

Vocational Developmental Stages and Substages

Stage 1: Growth, Ages Zero to Fifteen

This is characterized by the development during childhood of self-concept, attitudes, needs, and a general understanding of the work world. During this stage, the major developmental task is to develop a self-concept and then move from play to a work orientation.

Substages

- Fantasy (Ages Four to Ten): needs dominant career fantasies with little reality orientation
- Interest (Ages Eleven to Twelve): identifies likes/dislikes as a basis for career choices
- Capacity (Ages Thirteen to Fourteen): more reality is incorporated; can relate their own skills to specific job requirements

Stage 2: Exploration, Ages Fifteen to Twenty-Four

Characterized by exploration through classes, work experiences, and hobbies. During this stage, the young adult begins to make tentative choices and develop skills. The major tasks are to develop a realistic self-concept and to implement a vocational preference though role tryouts and exploration. During this stage, choices begin to narrow and more specific preferences develop.

Substages

- Tentative (Ages Fifteen to Seventeen): needs, interests, and abilities are exercised in fantasy, coursework, part-time work, volunteering, and job shadowing; may identify field and level of work at this substage

Stage 3: Establishment, Ages Twenty-Five to Forty-Four

This is characterized by entry-level skill building and stabilization through work experience. The task is to find a niche in a field and advance within it.

Substages

- Trial and Stabilization (Ages Twenty-Five to Thirty): process of starting professional work; if found to be unsatisfactory, can make additional job changes
- Advancement (Ages Thirty to Forty): efforts are directed at securing a position, acquiring seniority, developing skills, and demonstrating superior performance

Stage 4: Maintenance, Ages Forty-Five to Sixty-Four

This stage is characterized by a continual adjustment process to improve their position. The major task is to preserve the gains already made and develop non-work interests. Established work patterns are maintained.

Stage 5: Decline, Age Sixty-Five and Older

This is characterized by reduced output and the preparation for retirement. Major tasks include deceleration of a career, gradual disengagement from the work world, and eventual retirement. The individual is challenged to find other sources of satisfaction. At this time, their capacity to work can decline, making retirement or a shift away from work necessary.

Super's Archway Model, Life Career Rainbow, and Career Pattern Study

Donald Super created the Archway Model, which was illustrated as the Life Career Rainbow. This theory recognized the importance of a sense of self that could change over time and influence career choices. The model took into consideration lifestyle factors that included environmental (such as the labor market), personal (psychological and biological), and situational (socioeconomic) determinants. The Life Career Rainbow was represented by colored bands. It brought together the roles played in life (the "life-space/life roles") with the five developmental stages or structures of life (the "life span"). Super believed a person's self-concept developed as a result of the influence of the life roles played over a life span. His Career Pattern Study was longitudinal in nature and followed individuals over approximately fifteen years. The study's findings indicated that if individuals were successful in their high school years, they were also likely to be successful in young adulthood.

Life-Space and Life Roles

Within the Life Career Rainbow, life roles were included in what Donald Super called the life-space. The horizontal arches of the rainbow represented this life-space. Super believed that the role of "worker" was just one of many that an individual played in their lifetime, and they could play several roles at any given time. Throughout life, an individual's focus and attention could shift from one role to another, and work roles could develop throughout their lifespan. This theory was important because it focused on fitting work into their lives, as opposed to fitting individuals into jobs.

The life roles that Super defined were the:

- Child: spends time and energy on relationships with parents or guardians
- Student: focuses on education and training
- Leisurite: a term that Super coined for those who spend time and energy on hobbies and interests
- Citizen: focuses time and energy on civic, school, church, or political activities, which includes any community involvement or volunteer work
- Worker: spends time and energy on work for pay
- Parent: spends time and energy on child rearing, specifically in their younger years
- Spouse: role concentrates on relationships with their wife/husband/partner
- Homemaker: focuses on responsibility for home maintenance and management of the household.

Holland's Theory and Hexagon

Holland developed a theory in which personality was the basic factor in career choice. He created the Vocational Preference Inventory and Self-Directed Search (SDS) to assess traits and match them with specific occupations. He believed that individuals want careers with like-minded others of similar personalities. Most individuals fall into at least one of six personality types (depicted by a hexagon), which show the correlation between jobs and personality traits.

Holland's Six Personality Types

Realistic types enjoy working with their hands: building, fixing, assembling, and operating tools and equipment. These personalities can enjoy working outdoors. Occupations of interest include engineer, mechanic, pilot, electrician, computer technologist, sportsperson, and park ranger.

Investigative types enjoy problem solving, research, and discovery. These personalities like to observe, investigate, and experiment. Investigative individuals have excellent analytical, communication, and calculation skills. They can be best suited for careers in science, which include medical, health, and research occupations.

Artistic types express themselves through art, music, drama, and creative design. They enjoy performing, singing, dancing, planning, and presenting. Occupations of interest include artist, illustrator, fashion designer, photographer, and musician.

Social types like working with people. These personalities enjoy meeting new people, teaching, training, and coaching. They are skilled at treating others (as in a health setting) as well as providing care and support. Careers of interest can include athletic trainer, nurse, counselor, social worker, and dental hygienist.

Enterprising types like to meet people and enjoy working in business. They like talking, leading people, influencing, and encouraging others. These personalities are skilled at organizing, planning, developing, selling, promoting, and persuading. Careers of interest include lawyer, accountant, promoter, entrepreneur, manager, and business owner.

Conventional types like working with data and numbers. They enjoy accuracy, organization, and clear procedures. Conventional types are skilled at tasks that require orientation to detail. They excel at recordkeeping, handling money, working independently, and organization. Occupations of interest include librarian, office worker, bank clerk, and computer operator.

Krumboltz's Learning Theory of Career Counseling

Theorists Mitchell, Gelatt, and Krumboltz developed a career theory that demonstrated that learning occurs through both observations and experiences. This Learning Theory suggested that a career choice was based primarily on life events and four specific factors. Those factors are:

- Inherited Qualities: Genetic endowments and special abilities that could influence opportunity.

- Environmental Factors: Specific events and circumstances that influenced career preferences, skills development, and abilities. These were often out of an individual's control. Such factors could include access to education, resources, and socioeconomic conditions.

- Learning Experiences: Instrumental learning (reinforced by consequences) and associative learning (pairing a previously neutral situation with one that's positive or negative) about career options, and how certain choices could be rejected or reinforced by others.

- Task Approach Skills: Sets of skills the individual has developed, such as problem solving, work habits, mindsets, emotional response, and cognitive responses.

Krumboltz believed that the learning experiences individuals gain over their life span are the primary influences on their career choice. Using this model, counselors can help clients to understand the impact of external factors on their career path, recognize and manage the anxiety associated with not meeting their career goals, and choose alternative career paths. Krumboltz later developed a theory called Planned Happenstance, which suggested there were many factors in life outside of an individual's control. These factors could have both positive and negative impacts, and could help develop essential coping skills. This model taught counselors how to respond positively to clients and helped clients build

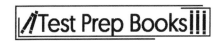

skills such as curiosity, persistence, flexibility, optimism, and risk-taking. By developing these skills, clients could react more positively to life events and create opportunities from negative situations.

Circumscription and Compromise Theory of Career Development

In 1981, Linda Gottfredson published a career theory based on the following processes of development: cognitive growth, development of self-concept, circumscription, and compromise. These processes guide how careers are chosen and occur over the first two decades of life.

Cognitive growth occurs as children begin to understand the distinctions between people and occupations. As adolescents, they develop a cognitive map to further distinguish occupations by gender and prestige.

Self-concept develops because personalities, interests, and traits reveal themselves as children experience the world. As this "self-concept" develops, children are naturally drawn to or repulsed by certain experiences and activities, and begin to create a niche for themselves.

Circumscription is a four-stage process of eliminating career options. These stages are:

Stage 1
Orientation to Size and Power (Ages Three to Five): As very young children, this first stage is about making simple observations and judgments on themselves and on adults. They begin to understand that adults have jobs and power. At this age, children stop referencing fantasy careers (such as being animals and superheroes) and begin to see the differences between the roles of children and adults.

Stage 2
Orientation to Sex Roles (Ages Six to Eight): During this stage, broad generalizations are made about gender roles as they relate to career choices. There can be a limited understanding of social hierarchies and what jobs are most lucrative; however, children can develop a simple understanding of social status and wealth. Decisions at this stage are mostly related to what's acceptable by gender, and occupations are eliminated if they don't match their defined gender concept.

Stage 3
Orientation to Social Valuation (Ages Nine to Thirteen): During this stage, children develop a more in-depth understanding of how specific occupations have a higher or lower status and, therefore, earn more or less money accordingly. They can see the relationship between types of jobs, money earned, and social rankings. Children may start to make decisions based on the level of effort required for some careers (e.g., being a doctor requires a high level) along with the status level they desire. They then begin to develop more realistic expectations based on these factors.

Stage 4
Orientation to Unique, Internal Self (Age Fourteen and Older): In the final stage, teens and young adults look internally more to determine which jobs fit their needs and personality. Prior to this stage, much of the learning and decision-making were external and status-based. This stage is far more complex as individuals now look at gender role, self-concept, status, and attainability of careers.

Compromise is the final stage. It takes into consideration factors outside of an individual's control, such as job availability, labor market conditions, and access to education and resources. Individuals may need to compromise on choices based on what's realistically available to them. During this stage, they will choose lower-level work or a different field before compromising their gender self-concept.

Roe's Career Development Theory

Anne Roe was influenced by Maslow's Hierarchy of Needs and developed a deterministic theory focusing on the relationship between occupational choice and personality. Roe believed psychological needs and parenting styles influenced career choices. Roe's Career Choice and Development Theory stated that specific parenting styles determined career paths. Cold and rejecting parents produced children interested in science and technology, while children of warm and accepting parents became interested in people-oriented jobs. Overprotective parents taught children to emphasize the speed at which their needs were met. Children of avoidant parents became unable to get their own needs met, while children of accepting parents understood how to be self-sufficient in meeting their own needs.

Roe developed eight occupational classifications, or *fields*: Service, Business, Organization, Technology, Outdoor, Science, General Culture, and Arts and Entertainment. These eight groups were separated into six rows, which represented six different levels of complexity and responsibility for each occupation. Roe stressed that the observable personality determined the career choice. These are also known as "fields and levels."

Theory of Ginzberg, Ginsburg, Axelrad, and Herma

In 1951, Ginzberg, Ginsburg, Axelrad, and Herma introduced a theory on career development as a lifelong process. Though this was one of the first developmental career theories, it was overshadowed by those of Super and others. Ginzburg, Ginsburg, Axelrad, and Herma believed vocational choice was influenced by reality, the educational process, emotions, and individual values. It was through three stages and substages that an individual would arrive at a career choice.

The Stages of Career Development are as follows:

- Fantasy (Up to Age Eleven): Children believe they can do anything and "play" at occupations of interest.
- Tentative (Ages Eleven to Seventeen): As adolescents, they begin to identify their interests, skills, abilities, and talents. They start to understand the education and training needed for certain careers.
- Realistic (Age Seventeen to Young Adulthood): There are three phases of this stage, during which young adults begin to make career decisions. The three substages are:
  o Exploration: restrict choices based on interests, abilities, and skills
  o Crystallization: make an occupational choice
  o Specification: pursue training or education required to meet their goal

Cognitive Information Processing (CIP) Career Development Theory

Cognitive Information Processing (CIP) was developed at Florida State University by researchers Peterson, Sampson, Reardon, and Lenz. It was based on the principles of Cognitive Therapy. CIP asserts that content and process are the main components of the career decision-making process. The content is what an individual must know to make a decision (e.g., self-assessment, knowledge of careers and options, etc.). The process is what an individual must do to make a decision.

The theory is represented by a pyramid, with the base being knowledge of the self and occupations. The center portion represents decision-making, which is made up of five information-processing skills:

- Communication
- Analysis
- Synthesis
- Valuing
- Executing

The top of the pyramid is metacognitions and the executive processing domain, which helps the individual evaluate decisions to determine their effectiveness. CIP is considered a practical method of career counseling that allows clients to be self-directed.

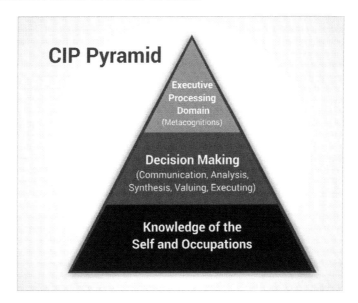

Tiedeman and O'Hara's Decision-Making Model

Tiedeman and O'Hara created a developmental model career theory based on Erik Erikson's eight stages of psychosocial development. They believed that the essential components to career choice were self-awareness and the learned ability to make decisions. Their assumption was that the world was not deterministic, and each person was responsible for their own behavior and choices. The three concepts that defined their theory were:

- Differentiation: expression of each person's unique individuality
- Integration: adjusting the person's individuality to fit in with society
- Ego Identity: a combination of the person's individuality and the need to integrate into society on a higher level

Tiedeman and O'Hara hypothesized two steps to making a career choice: Anticipation and Adjustment. During the Anticipation phase, a person engaged in Exploration to try new activities and fantasize about careers. This was followed by the Crystallization phase, when the person evaluated choices and began to clarify which vocations to pursue. Next, the individual made a Choice, and then finally engaged in Specification to reassess their decision.

The second step, Adjustment, had three phases that described adjusting to their choice of career. During the Induction phase, the new career choice was implemented. Next, the individual adjusted to new situations and people during the Reformation stage. Finally, Integration occurs as the individuals gained comfort and familiarity with the new environment.

The work of Tiedeman and O'Hara was the basis for Miller-Tiedeman's and Tiedeman's later theories. These theories were more holistic, and placed the client, not the career practitioner, in charge of creating their own career theory. This "life is career" theory embraced the process, leaving the development of content up to the individual.

Constructivism and Contextualism Approaches to Career Development

There are several postmodern approaches to career development that include theories on constructivism and contextualism. The constructivist approach suggests that reality is "constructed" by each individual (from the inside out) through cognitions and thought processes. In this theory, a person is constantly changing, and there are no developmental stages. The focus of development is on the process, not the outcome.

The contextualism approach focuses on individuals interacting within social and environmental contexts. This theory uses narratives to assist clients by helping them extract personal meaning from situations.

Social Cognitive Theory of Career Development

The social cognitive theory of career development was developed in 1994 by Lent, Brown, and Hackett and was based on Bandura's Social Cognitive theory. It explored the ways that academic and career choices develop and how choices are put into action. The theory was based on three principles: self-efficacy, outcome expectations, and goals. Self-efficacy relates to an individual's beliefs about the abilities they've gained from personal performance, learning, and social interactions. Outcome expectations are the beliefs in the consequences of behaviors and the effort an individual puts into specific activities. Personal success is defined by social efficacy (beliefs) and outcome expectations (effort and results). Finally, goals help to reinforce specific behaviors that lead to successful academic or career outcomes.

Sociological Model of Career Development

Unlike psychological theories that focus on the impact of personal characteristics, the sociological model considers the environmental and situational determinants of the individual. Sociological models study the impact of social systems, socioeconomic status, and the availability of training, resources, and jobs. The theory also factors in cultural and ethnic influences, as well as the occupations of parents and peers. Taking into consideration an individual's situation, choices can be determined by interests as well as by job market limitations and the lack of access to opportunity.

The Career Development Theory of John Crites

John Crites was influenced by both trait and factor theories and developmental theories. He synthesized several ideas to form his own model of career development. Crites's main concerns were types of diagnosis, the counseling process, and outcomes. The three diagnosis types were: differential (define the problem), dynamic (attempt to understand reasons for the problem), and decisional (how to deal with the problem). Crites developed a Career Maturity Inventory, which assisted counselors in assessing the level of career maturity. This concept indicated how well an individual could acknowledge and

understand information about themselves, their decision-making skills, and the world. The Career Maturity Inventory is believed to influence an individual's level of career success.

Limitations of Career Theories

Despite the volumes and varying perspectives of career theories, there are limitations to their scope and efficacy across all groups. Most theories address specific aspects of career development, but are not comprehensive. Many career research studies conducted in the 1950s and 1960s used a very limited sample set of middle class, white male college (or college-ready) students. Women, minorities, and cultural variations were not considered. For example, Holland's work has been extensively researched and revised to reduce gender bias. There also continues to be a debate over the validity of Holland's RIASEC types across nationalities and age groups. Newer theories factor in a more holistic approach and have a broader cultural understanding that considers the client's unique situations and needs.

Considerations When Providing Counseling Services

Adults with Disabilities

Individuals with disabilities have additional challenges in the career planning process. Disabilities include physical limitations, learning disabilities, cognitive impairment, mental health issues, as well as veterans in the Wounded Warrior class. Fortunately there are many resources available, including the Americans with Disabilities Act, the Job Accommodation Network (JAN), the Department of Labor **Disability Employment** Policy (ODEP), and many other national and community programs. Counselors can help clients to understand their legal rights and to learn how to educate employers about options during the application and interview process. Many employers can (and are required by law to) offer accommodations to assist with employment opportunity. In addition, most areas have service organizations that assist with career planning and can even offer on-the-job coaching.

Sexual Orientation

In recent years, there's been increased awareness and sensitivity to lesbian, gay, bisexual, and transgender (LGBT) individuals. However, like any minority group, they can be subject to discrimination and bias. For counselors, it's essential to be aware of LGBT issues in career development. Discrimination can occur in the interview process and on the job, and many states and countries don't provide legal protection to LGBT employees. An increasing number of employers value diversity in their workforce, and an April 2013 study shows that 88% of Fortune 500 companies enforce non-discrimination policies. Counselors working with LGBT individuals can utilize several strategies to increase the effectiveness of counseling. Making clients feel safe by demonstrating an understanding of LGBT culture is important, as well as avoiding stereotyping. Counselors should consult with other professionals as needed, use current resources on LGBT society, and refer out when necessary. Lastly, counselors should engage in open discussions about LGBT issues and help each client develop career goals unique to their personal situation.

World-of-Work Map

The World-of-Work Map illustrates the relationships between occupations, which assists counselors and students/job seekers in career exploration. It is visual and interactive, displaying similarities and differences between occupations. The map is similar to a pie chart, and the outer ring represents high-level tasks that correlate to Holland's RIASEC codes. There are four tasks for all combinations of people, ideas, things, and data. The map organizes 555 occupations into twenty-six groups of similar

occupations. Individuals can complete an ACT Interest Inventory to suggest map regions and career areas to explore.

Internet Resources

Currently, the career planning and job search process is almost entirely online. Most employers post jobs on their websites or via job boards, and many use Applicant Tracking Systems to receive and manage resumes. Job seekers and career professionals need a level of technical skill to manage this process and compete in the job market. There are a variety of general job search boards, including Indeed.com, USAJobs, CareerBuilder, Monster, and Job.com. In addition, there are many specialized sites for veterans, technical careers, healthcare, education, and more. There are also sites with extensive career resources, such as The Riley Guide and Quint Careers. Networking is still a critical part of the job search, and it has moved online via sites like LinkedIn, which has over 400 million members.

Occupational Outlook Handbook (OOH)

The Occupational Outlook Handbook (OOH) is a guide on labor economics and statistics that's designed for consumer use. It's a comprehensive source of information on occupations, which includes duties, education and training requirements, salaries, growth rates, and job outlook. The OOH is produced by the Bureau of Labor Statistics (a unit of the U.S. Department of Labor) and can be found at bls.gov.ooh. The handbook also includes information on highest-paying and fastest-growing careers, occupations projected to have the newest job openings, additional resources for teachers, a glossary of career terms, and career articles.

The Guide for Occupational Exploration (GOE)

The Guide for Occupational Exploration (GOE) is a printed resource based on the sixteen U.S. Department of Education clusters that connect learning to careers. The new GOE manual contains over 900 job descriptions from O*NET. It outlines skills needed, related courses, education required, earnings, and growth, and is helpful for career-path planning.

Workforce Innovation and Opportunity Act

The Workforce Innovation and Opportunity Act was enacted in 2014 and signed into law in 2016. It was designed to streamline training programs, and updated the 1998 version. Several agencies (including the Department of Labor), in coordination with the U.S. Department of Education and the U.S. Department of Health and Human Services, provide resources and support to ensure implementation. The new program is designed to help job seekers access employment, education, training, and support services. The goal is to increase services to the most economically challenged, including veterans, at-risk youth, and individuals with disabilities.

1994 School-to-Work Opportunities Act

This federal act was designed to support education at the state level. All fifty states received funding to help students succeed by engaging more with academics and learning to apply their education to the workforce. This program ended in 2001.

The Hidden Job Market

The *hidden job market* is a term used for jobs that aren't advertised. Employers attempt to fill these openings through referrals, so networking is considered the most effective way to get the job. Although difficult to quantify, it's believed that 60 percent or more of all jobs are filled through the hidden job market.

Dictionary of Occupational Titles (DOT) and O*Net

From the 1930s to the 1990s, the Dictionary of Occupational Titles (DOT) was the primary reference to define the specifics of occupations. This resource was often used in Worker's Compensation cases since it clearly outlined the physical requirements of thousands of occupations. It was eventually replaced by O*Net (Occupational Information Network), which is available at www.onetonline.org. O*Net provides tools and resources for career exploration, and includes an assessment that gives users Holland Codes and related occupations. The site is continually updated with information that's provided directly by professionals in the field. Specific areas of interest include: a My Next Move section for veterans; a Hot Technologies list; and the ability to search by keyword or SOC (Standard Occupational Classification) code.

Counseling Dual-Career/Dual-Earner Couples

In almost half of all American married couples, both individuals are employed. From 1996 to 2000 this number increased by 16 percent, making these dual-career couples (formerly an exception) more of a rule. Dual-career couples or families face the additional challenges of balancing work and home and, in many cases, parenting. Specific issues for working couples include: determining whose career is the "primary" or more important one, dividing household responsibilities, time-management, and stress. In some situations, one spouse is living part-time in another location (known as a commuter marriage) or is required to relocate, which means their spouse then follows them (known as a trailing spouse). Career counseling interventions for dual-career couples include open communication, clear expectations on both sides, support, and compromise.

Women in the Workforce

Since 1970, the number of women in the U.S. workforce has increased steadily from 38 percent to 47 percent of all workers, though the rate of growth has slowed in recent years. Women are earning secondary degrees at a faster rate than men, yet a wage difference between the genders still persists. Women currently represent over 72 million workers, while there are 81 million working men. On average, women earn approximately 80 percent of the wages of men. Leading occupations for women haven't changed considerably since the 1970s, with the majority of females working in secretarial/administrative roles and in education. The greatest growth of opportunities for female workers has been in the medical/healthcare sector, with occupations such as dentist, physician, veterinarian, and surgeon.

Managing families and children is another challenge women face. The U.S. is one of the few industrialized nations that doesn't offer paid maternity leave. In 2011, however, 16 percent of companies surveyed offered paid maternity leave, and 25 percent offered paid family leave. Overall, 70 percent of mothers work; 60 percent of women with children under three years of age and 55 percent of women with children under the age of one participate in the labor force.

Outsourcing

Outsourcing is a practice where companies transfer work to outside suppliers to reduce costs. This can involve manufacturing services and digital outsourcing, which can include call centers and technology services. One reason for outsourcing technology is that the wages of non-U.S. based technical professionals are far less. Outsourcing manufacturing can save on costs, including labor, utilities, and materials. Offshoring is the term for companies that move operations to another country. Outsourcing can also apply to the process of giving control of a public company to a private one. Outsourcing is complex and has both advantages and disadvantages for the U.S., the global economy, and workers.

Self-Directed Search (SDS)

Created by John Holland, the Self-Directed Search (SDS) is a career assessment tool that is available online. It allows the user to answer questions about interests, aspirations, activities, and skills, and to explore careers of interest. The current edition of the SDS is marketed to all segments of the population, including students, military and veterans, career changers, and retired workers. In addition, there are resources career counselors and Human Resources professionals can use to support clients in taking the assessment. Once completed, users receive their three-letter code, details on each type, and a list of corresponding occupations. In addition, users receive information on paths of study, leisure activities, and guidance on resources and next steps.

Theories of Mark Savickas and H.B Gelatt

Mark Savickas initially worked under Donald Super. Later, Savickas developed his own more post-modern views on career development. His belief was that the world had changed considerably since the initial ideas of Parsons and Super, so career development processes should change as well. He voiced criticism over assessments such as the Myers-Briggs Type Inventory (MBTI) and the SDS or other Holland Code-based tests, arguing that a letter code can't define an individual. He believed that individuals create their own reality and personal opinion of any career test results.

H.B Gelatt and his wife Carol Gelatt developed a career-related philosophy of Positive Uncertainty. The philosophy required a paradoxical approach to decision-making: accepting the uncertainty of the future, and being positive that it's uncertain. The Gelatts proposed four principles to decision-making:

- Be focused and flexible about what you want.
- Be aware and wary about what you know.
- Be realistic and optimistic about what you believe.
- Be practical and magical about what you do to decide.

Using this process of embracing uncertainty and positivity can provide the opportunity for proactive creativity. Since the future is uncertain, attitudes and beliefs can influence outcomes and help an individual create their desired future.

Self-Efficacy Theory

Based on Bandura's work, self-efficacy theories refer to an individual's belief in their ability to succeed in specific situations or to accomplish specific tasks. It also refers to confidence in their abilities, and the motivation to persist at a task or process. Career self-efficacy was studied by Nancy Betz and Gail Hackett in the 1980s and explained how individuals performed tasks such as choosing and adjusting to

careers. Low career self-efficacy causes an individual to avoid career decisions, procrastinate, and be lacking in motivation. Those with high self-efficacy are more adept at envisioning success, taking on challenges, and committing to outcomes.

Undecided vs. Indecisive

Although similar, these terms have different meanings, particularly when applied to career decision-making:

- Undecided: Being undecided can be a normal part of the career development process. Individuals may need additional education or information to make a career choice.

- Indecisive: Being indecisive is a more global concern. This is where an individual can't make decisions, even when presented with available information and adequate resources.

Compensatory vs. Spillover Theories of Leisure

There are two competing theories on the meaning of "time outside of work." The spillover theory suggests carry-over and similar patterning between work and non-work activities. The compensatory theory suggests the opposite, arguing that individuals are more interested in leisure that's unlike their work, and uses the negative association with work to fulfill their non-work needs. Research has indicated slightly more evidence of spillover than compensatory.

Career Guidance vs. Career Counseling

Career Guidance is the process of helping individuals make educational, training, and occupational decisions. Career Counseling is a more individualized and complex approach of working with all of the factors that can impact the career development process. This can include self-assessment, job search, career exploration or change, work/life balance, and transitions.

Competencies Expected

Career counselors should have a broad range of helping, facilitating, coaching, training, and communication skills. These include:

- Knowledge of and training with career assessment tools
- An understanding of personality and career theories that impact development, motivation, decision-making, and choices
- Excellent communication skills, including the ability to interpret meanings across cultures
- The ability to counsel individuals and groups
- Knowledge of and sensitivity to diversity, including cultural, racial, sexual orientation, economic, and family status
- Knowledge of the job search market and effective self-marketing (for example, job search correspondence such as resumes and cover letters)
- An understanding of social media and its impact on employment
- Technical skills
- The ability to research career options and teach others to perform research

Career Counseling Process

The career counseling process typically begins with an intake review to understand the individual's goals for counseling. Career assessments can be provided and then interpreted by the counselor. Sessions can be conducted to review and discuss the outcomes of these assessments. The counselor works with the client to establish goals and outline a timeline that's suitable for both of them. Sessions continue until the client reaches or updates their goals. Career counseling is typically solution-focused and time-limited.

Counseling Adults in Career Transition

Although many theories focus on the career decision-making process of young adults, career development is a lifelong process. At any stage in life, adults may need career guidance or counseling to assist with transitions. These transitions include career changes, lay-offs, the need for additional education or training, returning to work after time off (for raising children or caring for family members), and retirement. The job search process has changed dramatically, and older workers may need assistance navigating technology to search for jobs.

Areas of Assessment

The process of career exploration includes helping an individual discover their career values, interests, skills, and personality. Assessment tools can also explore motivation, aptitude, and work preferences. Validated assessments and their focus include:

- Strong Interest Inventory (SII) (Interests): provides Holland Codes and occupational matches
- Self-Directed Search (SDS): shorter version of the SII
- O*Net Interest Profiler (Interests): available online
- Career Assessment Inventory (Interests): for college- and non-college-bound individuals
- Myers-Briggs Type Indicator (Personality): provides a four-letter personality code and career areas of fit
- Work Preference Inventory (Work Styles/Interests): measures motivation towards work
- Minnesota Importance Questionnaire (Values): measures work needs and values
- Super's Work Values Inventory (Values): measures work-related values
- Kuder Career Interests Assessment (Interests, Skills and Values): includes Skills Confidence and Work Values
- Armed Services Vocational Aptitude Battery (ASVAB): predicts academic and occupational success in the military

Computer-Assisted Career Guidance Systems (CACGSs)

Although a variety of career assessments are available online, validated and reliable versions require administration and interpretation by a trained professional. Some online assessments can lack validity and provide only basic information on interests and options. There are vast amounts of career resources available online, including articles, tutorials, job search sites, resume writing programs, videos, and podcasts. Some computer-based programs have become obsolete due to rapidly changing technology. The System of Interactive Guidance Information (SIGI) is a computer-assisted career guidance system (CACGS) for university students and adults. It is still in use and rated highly by both users and career professionals. DISCOVER, another CACGS, allows students to access information and resources related to their career development. This includes self-assessment tools, occupations, information on majors,

resources for financing the cost of higher education, and job search tools. The Choices Planner helps students explore career options and is available through Bridges Transitions. The Kiersey Temperament Sorter is available online and defines temperament and behavior based on Myers-Briggs Type Indications. Focus 2, initially developed in 1967 as an Education & Career Exploration System (ECES), was renamed in 1990 and continues to be used for career and major exploration and decision-making. Career OneStop, a career exploration and job search site sponsored by the Department of Labor, contains a variety of assessment tools.

Important Terms

Career Education: broadly refers to programs designed to help students understand vocational options, including college, training schools, and other non-skilled occupations

Career Exploration: process of exploring career options through various self-assessment tools

Dislocated Worker: anyone who becomes unemployed as a result of downsizing, layoffs, company relocation, or company closing

Displaced Homemaker: a parent who begins or returns to work after taking time off to care for a child; can be the result of a divorce or separation where the parent has a new financial need to support themselves

Externship: a short-term (several weeks) work experience that allows an individual to experience a specific work environment or job function

Family and Medical Leave Act (FMLA): the U.S. law passed in 1993 to provide support to working parents. The initial law covered time off of work for pregnancy, infant care, adoption, or medical care for an individual or their spouse, parent, or child. Additional time of up to twenty-six total weeks can be allowed if a spouse, parent, or child is active duty military and requires care for an illness or injury related to their service. The law was updated in 2015 to include same-sex married couples. It also protects individuals by allowing up to twelve weeks per year of unpaid leave with a continuation of health care coverage and the ability to return to the same or an equal job. FMLA applies to all public and private businesses, but a private employer must have a minimum of fifty employees to be required to offer FMLA.

Freelance: an option for more flexible work, but without any benefits. Individuals can freelance for one or more organizations to make additional money

Glass Ceiling: the term for an invisible cap on wages and the potential for advancement, particularly for women and minorities

Internship: a longer-term work experience. It can be paid or unpaid while providing experience with a specific job function, employer, or industry. Internships are most often completed by college students as part of a degree program.

Job Satisfaction: term for defining an individual's satisfaction with work, which includes the work, company, colleagues, compensation, value of work, and environment

Mentor: a higher-level individual (in a company or industry) offering career guidance and support. This is often a mutually beneficial relationship, providing personal growth for both parties.

Outplacement Counseling: career services for those who are laid off due to downsizing or company relocation

Personal Branding: used in conjunction with social media, this is a way for job seekers to describe and market themselves, demonstrating their unique value to employers

Portfolio Career: having multiple part-time/freelance jobs as opposed to one full-time job. This requires organization, flexibility, and risk tolerance.

Retirement Counseling: providing services to adults who are close to retirement to ensure they are financially and socially prepared

Re-Careering: a term coined for "Baby Boomers" making a late life career change before retiring

Social Networking: making connections to others through social media

Telecommuting: working from home (or another remote location) all or part of the time. This can help improve efficiency and reduce costs for the employer.

Underemployment: working at a job below one's educational or experience level

Work/Life Balance: prioritizing time spent on a career with time spent on lifestyle and leisure activities

Generational Differences

Currently, there are several distinct generational groups in the workforce. The Baby Boomer Generation consists of approximately 78 million individuals born between 1946 and 1964. Though many Baby Boomers are at or nearing retirement age, they can be at the peak of earning potential and want to delay retirement for financial reasons. The average age of retirement is now sixty-six, which is up from past years.

Generation Y (also known as the *Millennials*) represents 72 million individuals born between the late 1970s and the late 1990s. As job seekers and workers, this group has distinctly different views on the meanings and requirements of work. Overall, they desire increased flexibility, transparency with leadership, and work that has clear value. In addition, Millennials are highly socially conscious and tech-savvy. This generation will ultimately transform all aspects of employment as they age and move up the corporate ladder. In the meantime, companies should work to create cohesiveness and cooperation across generations with distinct differences.

Practice Questions

1. Who is considered "the father of the vocational guidance movement?"
    a. Jesse B. Davis
    b. Frank Parsons
    c. Donald Super
    d. John Holland

2. The 1944 "G.I. Bill" offered what services to soldiers returning from World War II?
    a. Free vocational assessments
    b. Support in joining the armed forces
    c. Teacher training
    d. Higher education and training options to veterans

3. The National Defense Education Act (NDEA) of 1958 was launched in response to what event?
    a. The launch of Sputnik by the USSR
    b. The end of World War II
    c. High unemployment of war veterans
    d. Concerns for acts of terror

4. In Donald Super's theory, there are three substages in Stage 1 of development, from ages four to fourteen. These include what?
    a. Fantasy, Interest, and Capacity
    b. Exploration, Fantasy, and Intent
    c. Exploration, Interest, and Maintenance
    d. Trial, Interest, and Stabilization

5. In adults, the Maintenance Stage is defined by what actions?
    a. Finding one's career niche and advancing
    b. Preserving gains and developing non-work interests
    c. Preparing for retirement
    d. Narrowing career choices

6. Super's Life Career Rainbow included what aspect(s) of development?
    a. Life roles
    b. Life-space
    c. Self-concept
    d. Choices A and B

7. Assessments developed by John Holland include which of the following?
    a. The Minnesota Occupational Rating Scale
    b. The Strong Interest Inventory, Self-Directed Search, and Vocational Preference Inventory
    c. The World-of-Work Map
    d. The Myers-Briggs Type Indicator

8. Limitations to early career theories included which of the following?
   a. A lack of studies of women and minorities
   b. Non-comprehensive theories
   c. A focus on white, educated males
   d. All of the above

9. Which of the following are included in Holland's Personality Types?
   a. Realistic, Investigative, and Social
   b. Creative, Social, and Enterprising
   c. Conventional, Realistic, and Helping
   d. Entrepreneurial, Social, and Artistic

10. Tiedeman and O'Hara's developmental model encompassed what three concepts?
    a. Id, Ego, and Superego
    b. Id, Integration, and Superego
    c. Differentiation, Ego, and Ego Identity
    d. Differentiation, Integration, and Ego Identity

11. When working with individuals in the LGBT community, it's important for a counselor to do what?
    a. Be an active member of the LGBT community
    b. Assist the client in locating gender-neutral jobs
    c. Consult with other professionals and refer out when necessary
    d. Reach out to employers to provide education about discriminatory hiring practices

12. Krumboltz's theory of Planned Happenstance suggests which of the following?
    a. Many factors in life are outside of our control
    b. It's essential to develop coping skills
    c. Opportunity can be created from a negative situation
    d. All of the above

13. Positive Uncertainty is a paradoxical approach to decision-making. What are its two main beliefs?
    a. The future is uncertain, and one must be positive it's uncertain
    b. The future is certain, and must be accepted
    c. The future is uncertain, and anxiety is a natural result
    d. The future is unpredictable, and can be changed

14. A counselor would most likely fall into which of Holland's Personality Types?
    a. Realistic
    b. Helping
    c. Conventional
    d. Social

15. The hidden job market represents what percentage of open jobs?
    a. 20 percent
    b. 40 percent
    c. 50 percent
    d. 60 percent

16. The Dictionary of Occupational Titles (DOT) was replaced by what resource?
    a. The Self-Directed Search (SDS)
    b. The Occupational Outlook Handbook
    c. O*Net
    d. World-of-Work Map

17. The Baby Boomer generation represents which age group?
    a. Adults born 1956-1971
    b. Adults born 1976-1996
    c. Adults born 1936-1951
    d. Adults born 1946-1964

18. Which of the following does *outsourcing* refer to?
    a. Companies replacing U.S. workers with overseas workers
    b. Companies relocating outside of the U.S.
    c. Companies buying out smaller companies
    d. Working from home or a remote location

19. What are the main components of the Cognitive Information Processing (CIP) career development theory?
    a. Communication and Analysis
    b. Synthesis and Valuing
    c. Valuing and Executing
    d. Content and Process

20. Computer-Assisted Career Guidance Systems (CACGSs) include what?
    a. SIGI and DISCOVER
    b. The Kiersey Temperament Sorter and Myers-Briggs Type Inventory
    c. FOCUS2 and Choices
    d. Answers A and C

Answer Explanations

1. B: Frank Parsons was a key figure in the early years of vocational development and is considered "the father of vocational guidance movement." Jesse B. Davis, Choice *A*, was an educator who developed one of the first vocational guidance programs through teaching staff. Donald Super and John Holland, Choices *C* and *D*, were both career theorists.

2. D: The "G.I. Bill" was launched in 1944 to provide higher education and thus increased employment options for returning veterans. Returning veterans compounded U.S. unemployment as veterans displaced workers for available jobs.

3. A: The launch of Sputnik by the former USSR started the "space race" and spurred the U.S. to invest in science education. Funding from the act was used to provide career testing, hire and train school counselors, and encourage the study of science.

4. A: The three substages of Stage 1 are Fantasy, Interest, and Capacity. Exploration is Stage 2, making Choice *B* incorrect. Establishment is Stage 3, and Maintenance is Stage 4, making Choice *C* incorrect. Trial and stabilization occur within Stage 3, making Choice *D* incorrect.

5. B: In the maintenance phase (ages forty-five to sixty-four), adults work to preserve gains and develop non-work interests. Finding one's niche and advancing, Choice *A,* takes place during the Establishment phase (ages twenty-five to forty-four). Preparing for retirement, Choice *C,* occurs during the Decline phase (Age sixty-five and over) and narrowing of choices, Choice *D,* takes place in Stage 2, Exploration.

6. D: The Life Career Rainbow is represented by colored bands, and brings together the roles played in life (defined as the life-space/life roles) with the five developmental stages or structures of life (the life span). Donald Super believed a person's self-concept developed as a result of the influence the life roles played over a life span. Within the Life Career Rainbow, life roles are included in what Super called the life-space.

7. B: The correct answer is the Strong Interest Inventory, Self-Directed Search, and Vocational Preference Inventory. Donald Paterson published the Minnesota Occupational Rating Scale in 1953, so Choice *A* is incorrect. The World-of-Work Map, Choice *C*, is based on Holland Codes but wasn't developed by Holland. The Myers-Briggs Type Indicator, Choice *D*, was developed by Katharine Cook Briggs and her daughter Isabel Briggs Myers.

8. D: All of the above. Many career research studies conducted in the 1950s and 1960s used a very limited sample set of middle-class, white male college or college-ready students. Women, minorities, and cultural variations often weren't considered.

9. A: Holland Types are Realistic, Investigative, Artistic, Social, Enterprising, and Conventional (RIASEC). Holland developed a theory in which personality was the basic factor in career choice. Realistic types like working with their hands, investigative types enjoy problem solving, research, and discovery. Artistic types express themselves through art, music, drama, and creative design. Social types like working with people. Enterprising types like to meet people and enjoy working in business. Conventional types like working with data and numbers.

10. D: Tiedeman and O'Hara's three concepts are: Differentiation (how one expresses their individuality), Integration (the ability to be part of society by adjusting to others) and Ego Identity (personal meanings, values, and relationships that are the foundation for broader integration with society). Id, Ego, and Superego are all Freudian terms, making Choices *A, B,* and *C* incorrect.

11. C: It's important for a counselor to consult with other professionals if they feel they're outside the scope for their practice area. Being in the LGBT community is not necessary, although awareness and respect for the culture is.

12. D: Planned Happenstance suggests that much is out of our control, thus it's imperative to develop coping skills to deal with life changes. It also suggests opportunity can arise from various situations, including negative ones.

13. A: Positive uncertainty requires a paradoxical approach to decision-making: accepting the uncertainty of the future, and being positive that it's uncertain.

14. D: Social types would closely match the personality of a counselor. Helping, Choice *B*, is not a Holland Code. Realistic types like working with their hands so Choice *A* is incorrect. Conventional types, Choice *C*, like working with data and numbers, so this is also incorrect.

15. D: The hidden job market is a term for jobs that are unadvertised. Employers attempt to fill these openings through referrals. Thus, networking is still considered the most effective means to a job. Although difficult to quantify, it's believed 60 percent or more of all jobs are filled through the hidden job market.

16. C: The answer is O*Net. DOT provided vocational information from 1938 to 1999, but was then considered an obsolete print resource. It was replaced by the O*Net database. Choice *A*, Self-Directed Search, is a career assessment tool that is available online. Choice *B*, the Occupational Outlook Handbook, is a guide on labor economics and statistics that's designed for consumer use. Choice *D*, World-of-Work Map, illustrates the relationships between occupations, which assists counselors and students/job seekers in career exploration.

17. D: Adults fifty-two to seventy years of age. Baby Boomers were born during the post-World War II "baby boom" from 1946 to 1964.

18. A: Although a complex business topic, outsourcing typically refers to companies hiring non-U.S.-based workers to replace U.S. workers. It is thought to be a cost-saving measure, since wages in other countries can be far less.

19. D: Cognitive Information Processing (CIP) asserts that content and process are the main components of the career decision-making process. The content is what an individual must know to make a decision (such as self-assessment and knowledge of careers and options). The process is what an individual needs to do to make a decision.

20. D: SIGI, DISCOVER, FOCUS2, and Choices are all Computer-Assisted Career Guidance Systems (CACGSs). The Kiersey and Myers-Briggs can be taken online, but aren't considered computer assisted.

Assessment and Testing

Types of Reliability

Reliability in testing is the degree to which the assessment tool produces consistent and stable results. There are four types of reliability:

- Test-Retest Reliability involves administering the same test twice to a group of individuals, then correlating the scores to evaluate stability.

- Parallel-Forms Reliability (also referred to as *equivalence*) involves administering two different versions of an assessment that measure the same set of skills, knowledge, etc. and then correlating the results. A test can be written and split into two parts, thus creating parallel versions.

- Inter-Rater Reliability (also referred to as *inter-observer*) checks to see that raters (those administering, grading, or judging a measure) do so in agreement. Each rater should value the same measures and at the same degree to ensure consistency. Inter-rater reliability prevents overly subjective ratings, since each rater is measuring on the same terms.

- Internal Consistency refers to how well a test or assessment measures what it's intended to measure, while producing similar results each time. Questions on an assessment should be similar and in agreement, but not repetitive. High internal consistency indicates that a measure is reliable.

  - Average Inter-Item Correlation is used to determine if scores on one item relate to the scores on all of the other items in that scale. Ensuring that each correlation between items is a form of redundancy to ensure the same content is assessed with each question.

  - Split-Half Reliability is the random division of questions into two sets. Results of both halves are compared to ensure correlation.

Validity

Validity refers to how well a test or assessment measures what it's intended to measure. For example, an assessment on depression should only measure the degree to which an individual meets the diagnostic criteria for depression. Though validity does indicate reliability, a test can be reliable but not be valid. There are four major types of validity, with subtypes:

- Content Validity ensures that the test questions align with the content or study area. This can be measured by two subtypes of validation:

  - Face Validity refers to a commonsense view that a test measures what it should and looks accurate from a non-professional viewpoint.

  - Curricular Validity is evaluated by experts, and measures that a test aligns with the curriculum being tested. For example, a high school exit exam measures the information taught in the high school curriculum.

- Criterion Validity measures success and the relationship between a test score and an outcome, such as scores on the SAT and success in college. It's two subtypes are:

  o Predictive Validity refers to how useful test scores are at predicting future performance.

  o Concurrent Validity is used to determine if measures can be substituted, such as taking an exam in place of a class. Measures must take place concurrently to accurately test for validity.

- Construct Validity refers to a test that measures abstract traits or theories, and isn't inadvertently testing another variable. For example, a math test with complex word problems may be assessing reading skills. Two subtypes of validation are needed to assess construct validity:

  o Convergent Validity uses two sets of tests to determine that the same attributes are being measured and correlated. For example, two separate tests can measure students similarly.

  o Discriminant Validity refers to using tests that measure differently and results that don't correlate.

- Consequential Validity refers to the social consequences of testing. Though not all researchers feel it's a true measure of validity, some believe a test must benefit society in order to be considered valid.

Administering Tests to Clients

As part of the counseling process, it can be necessary for the counselor to administer tests or assessments to measure and evaluate the client. Tests are a more formalized means to quantify information and guide treatment options, or to develop goals. Assessments are more informal. They can include surveys, interviews, and observations. There are a variety of reasons a counselor can choose to administer a test or assessment, such as to:

- Help the client gain a better understanding of themselves
- Provide counselors with concrete data
- Ensure a client's needs are within the counselor's scope of practice
- Assist in decision-making and goal-setting for the counseling process
- Provide insight to both the client and the counselor
- Assist in setting clear expectations for clients
- Help the counselor gain a deeper understanding of their client's needs
- Set benchmarks to ensure client and counselor are making progress towards their goals
- Evaluate the effectiveness of counseling interventions

Interpreting Test Scores

To begin, any test or assessment should be given under controlled circumstances. The counselor should follow any instructions provided in the test manual. Once completed, the counselor and client can discuss the results.

Some best practices for interpreting results are listed below:

- Counselor must thoroughly understand the results
- Counselor should explain results in easily understood terms, and be able to provide supporting details and norms as needed
- Counselor should explain and understand average scores and the meanings of results
- Counselor should allow the client to ask questions and review aspects of the test to ensure understanding
- Counselor must explain the ramifications and limitations of any data obtained through testing

Major Types of Tests and Inventories

Achievement tests measure knowledge of a specific subject and are primarily used in education. Examples include exit exams for high school diplomas and tests used in the Common Core for educational standards. The General Education Development (GED) and the California Achievement Test are both achievement tests that measure learning.

Aptitude tests measure the capacity for learning and can be used as part of a job application. These tests can measure abstract/conceptual reasoning, verbal reasoning, and/or numerical reasoning. Examples include the Wonderlic Cognitive Ability Test, the Differential Aptitude Test (DAT), the Minnesota Clerical Test, and the Career Ability Placement Survey (CAPS).

Intelligence tests measure mental capability and potential. One example is the Wechsler Adult Intelligence Scale (WAIS-IV), currently in its fourth edition. The Wechsler Intelligence Scale for Children (WISC-IV), also in its fourth edition, is used for children six years of age to sixteen years eleven months of age, and can be completed without reading or writing. There's a separate version of the test for children aged two years six months to seven years seven months, known as the Wechsler Preschool and Primary Scale of Intelligence (WPPSI-III). Examples of other intelligence tests are the Stanford-Binet Intelligence Scale, the Woodcock-Johnson Tests of Cognitive Abilities, and the Kaufman Assessment Battery for Children.

Occupational tests can assess skills, values, or interests as they relate to vocational and occupational choices. Examples include the Strong Interest Inventory, the Self-Directed Search, the O*Net Interest Profiler, the Career Assessment Inventory, and the Kuder Career Interests Assessment.

Personality tests can be objective (rating scale based) or projective (self-reporting based), and help the counselor and client understand personality traits and underlying beliefs and behaviors. The Myers-Briggs Type Inventory (MBTI) provides a specific psychological type, reflecting the work of Carl Jung. It's often used as part of the career development process. Other rating scale personality tests include the Minnesota Multiphasic Personality Inventory (MMPI-2), the Beck Depression Inventory, and the Tennessee Self-Concept Scale. The Rorschach (inkblot) and the Thematic Apperception Test are both projective tests, designed to reveal unconscious thoughts, motives, and views.

Ethical Issues in Testing

A variety of ethical issues must be considered before, during, and after any test or assessment is administered. To begin, the counselor must be adequately trained and earn any certifications and supervision necessary to administer and interpret the test. Tests must be appropriate for the needs of the specific client. Next, the client must provide informed consent, and they must understand the purpose and scope of any test. Test results must remain confidential, which includes access to any

virtual information. Finally, tests must be validated for the specific client and be unbiased toward the race, ethnicity, and gender of the client.

Key Contributors in the Field of Intelligence Testing

Sir Francis Galton, an English anthropologist and explorer, was one of the first individuals to study intelligence in the late 1800s. A cousin of Charles Darwin, Galton coined the term *eugenics* and believed that intelligence was genetically determined and could be promoted through selective parenting.

American psychologist J.P. Guilford conducted psychometric studies of human intelligence and creativity in the early 1900s. He believed intelligence tests were limited and overly one-dimensional, and didn't factor in the diversity of human abilities, thinking, and creativity.

English psychologist Charles Spearman was responsible for bringing statistical analysis to intelligence testing. In the early 1900s, Spearman proposed the g Factor Theory for general intelligence, which laid the foundation for analyzing intelligence tests. Prior to his work, tests weren't highly correlated with the factors they attempted to measure.

Also in the 1900s, French psychologist Alfred Binet, along with medical student Theodore Simon, developed the first test to determine which children would succeed in school. His initial test, the Binet-Simon, focused on the concept of mental age, and included memory, attention, and problem-solving skills. In 1916, Binet's work was brought to Stanford University and developed into the Stanford-Binet Intelligence Scale. It's since been revised multiple times and is still widely used.

In the 1940s, Raymond Cattell began developing theories on fluid and crystallized intelligence. His student, John Horn, continued this work. The Cattell-Horn Theory hypothesized that over one hundred abilities work together to create forms of intelligence. Fluid intelligence is defined as the ability to think and act quickly and to solve new problems, skills that are independent of education and enculturation. Crystallized intelligence encompasses acquired and learned skills, and is influenced by personality, motivation, education, and culture. In 1949, Catell and his wife, Alberta Karen Cattell, founded the Institute for Personality and Ability Testing at the University of Illinois. Cattell developed several assessments, including the 16 Personality Factor Questionnaire and the Culture Fair Intelligence Test.

In the 1950s, American psychologist David Wechsler developed intelligence tests for adults and children. His tests were adept at identifying learning disabilities in children. Wechsler began his career developing personality tests for the U.S. military. He disagreed with some aspects of the Stanford-Binet Intelligence Scale, and believed intelligence had both verbal and performance components. He also believed factors other than pure intellect influenced intellectual behavior. Wechsler's tests are still used today for adults, as well as school-age and primary-age children. They include the Wechsler Adult Intelligence Scale (WAIS-IV), the Wechsler Intelligence Scale for Children (WISC-IV), and the Wechsler Preschool and Primary Scale of Intelligence (WPPSI-III).

John Ertl, a professor working in Canada in the 1970s, invented a neural efficiency analyzer to more effectively measure intelligence. He believed traditional intelligence tests were limited to understanding an abstract degree of intelligence. Ertl's system measured the speed and efficiency of electrical activity in the brain using an electroencephalogram (EEG).

Arthur Jensen supported the g Factor Theory and believed intelligence consisted of two distinct sets of abilities. Level I accounted for simple associative learning and memory, while Level II involved more abstract and conceptual reasoning. Jensen also believed that genetic factors were the most influential indicator of intelligence. In 1998, he published the book *The g Factor: The Science of Mental Ability.*

Important Terms

Appraisal: professionally administered assessment tools and tests used to evaluate, measure, and understand clients

Behavioral Observation: type of assessment used to document the behavior of clients or research subjects

Bell Curve: illustration of data distribution that resembles the shape of a bell

Coefficient of Determination: denoted by R^2, the proportion of the variance in the dependent variable that's predictable from the independent variable and the square of the coefficient of correlation

Correlation Coefficient: statistic that describes the relationship between two variables and their impact on one another. In positive correlation, both variables react in the same direction. In negative correlation, variables react in opposite directions.

Dichotomous Items: opposing choices on a test, such as yes/no or true/false options

Difficulty Index: measure of the proportion of examinees who answer test items correctly

External Validity: describes how well results from a study can be generalized to the larger population

Forced Choice Items: the use of two or more specific response options on a survey

Free Choice Test: also known as *liberal choice*; questions that allow for a subjective/open-ended response

Halo Effect: an overgeneralized positive view of a person from limited data. An example of this would be favoring a politician for their attractiveness and assuming that attractiveness extends to their ethical beliefs or personality.

Horizontal Test: a test covering material across various subjects

Ipsative Format: means of testing that measures how individuals prefer to respond to problems, people, and procedures and doesn't compare results to others

Likert Scale: rating scale measuring attitudes to a degree of like or dislike

Mean: provides the average of all scores; calculated by adding all given test scores and dividing by the number of tests

Median: refers to the middle or center number in an ordered list of scores or data; also referred to as the midpoint. In an even data set, the two middle numbers are typically averaged to determine the median.

Measure: score assigned to traits, behaviors, or actions

Mode: the most common or frequent score that occurred in a group of tests. If a number/score doesn't occur twice, a test doesn't have a mode.

Normative Format: means of testing to compare individuals to others

Objective Test Items: standardized questions with clear correct or incorrect answers; not open to any interpretation

Obtrusive Measurement: assessment tools (such as observation) conducted without knowledge of the individual

Percentile: determines how test scores rank on a scale of 100. Percentiles determine the number of individuals who are at or below a given rank. For example, a test taker who scores in the 65th percentile performed better than 65 percent of the other test takers.

Projective Test: responses to ambiguous images that are intended to uncover unconscious desires, thoughts, or beliefs

Psychological Assessment: an informal process of testing, interviews, or observations used to determine the psychological needs of an individual. Assessments can expose the need for more formal testing.

Psychological Test: refers to any number of specific tests or measurements conducted to evaluate, diagnose, or develop treatment plans. It can include personality assessments, projective or subjective tests, intelligence tests, or diagnostic batteries.

Psychometrics: the process or study of psychological measurement

Q-Sort: self-assessment procedure requiring subjects to sort items relative to one another along a dimension, such as agree/disagree

Range: subtraction of the lowest score from the highest score

Rapport: development of trust, understanding, respect, and liking between two people; essential for an effective therapeutic relationship

Rating Scale: process of measuring degrees of experience and attitudes through questions

Regression to the Mean: statistical tendency of a data series to gravitate towards the center of a distribution

Reliability: four types of reliability are test-retest, parallel forms, inter-rater, and internal consistency. Each type measures that a tool is producing consistent and stable results that must be quantified. Reliability doesn't indicate validity.

Scale: used to categorize and/or quantify variables. The four scales of measurement are nominal, ordinal, interval, and ratio.

Score: numerical value associated with a test or measure

Skew: the measure a score deviates from the norm

Standard Deviation: measure of dispersion of numbers; calculated by the square root of the variance

Standard Error of Measurement (SEM): refers to test reliability and the difference between the true score versus the observed score. Since no test is without error, the SEM depicts the dispersion of scores of the same test to rule out errors, also referred to as the "standard error" of a score.

Subjective: individual perceptions/interpretations based on feelings and opinions, but not necessarily based on fact

Stanine (STAndard NINE): a nine-point scale used to convert a test score to a single digit. Stanines are always positive whole numbers from zero to nine.

T-Score: specific to psychometrics, used to standardize test scores and convert scores to positive numbers. T-Scores represent the number of standard deviations the score is from the mean (which is always fifty).

Test: a measuring device or procedure

Test Battery: a group or set of tests administered to the same group and scored against a standard

Trait: method of describing individuals through observable characteristics that are unique and distinguishable

Validity: indicates how well any given test or assessment measures what it's intended to measure. There are four major types of validity: content, construct, criterion, and consequential. Validity *does* indicate reliability.

Variance: how widely individuals in a group vary; how data is distributed from the mean and the square of the standard deviation

Vertical Test: same-subject tests given to different levels or ages

Z-Score: also referred to as a *standard score*, Z-Scores measure the number of standard deviations a raw score is from the mean. Z-scores use zero as the mean.

Practice Questions

1. Face validity is a subtype of content validity. Content validity ensures that the questions align with the content. What is face validity?
    a. Common sense
    b. Verifiable by professionals
    c. Measures success
    d. Measures abstract traits or theories

2. Which of the following is NOT a personality test?
    a. Minnesota Multiphasic Personality Inventory (MMPI-2)
    b. Beck Depression Inventory
    c. Stanford-Binet Intelligence Scale
    d. Myers-Briggs Type Inventory (MBTI)

3. Which of the following is the type of reliability that involves administering two different versions of an assessment that measures the same set of skills and then correlates the results?
    a. Internal Consistency
    b. Inter-Rater
    c. Test-Retest
    d. Parallel-Forms

4. What do achievement tests measure?
    a. Academic potential
    b. Unconscious behaviors
    c. Learning
    d. Intellectual capacity

5. Isabella is ready to join the workforce, but she is unsure what kind of job she would like. A friend recommends to Isabella a test that is used to assess what kind of career she might like or what kind of work she might be good at. What kind of test is Isabella's friend probably referring to?
    a. Intelligence Test
    b. Occupational Test
    c. Achievement Test
    d. Personality Test

6. Who was one of the first to measure intelligence by way of a structured test?
    a. Raymond Cattell
    b. Carl Jung
    c. Alfred Binet
    d. Sir Francis Galton

7. Which of the following is NOT reason a counselor would administer a test or assessment to a client?
    a. Aid the counselor in sharing pertinent information with the client's loved ones
    b. Ensure a client's needs are within the counselor's scope of practice
    c. Help the client gain a better understanding of themselves
    d. Evaluate the effectiveness of counseling interventions

8. Predictive validity is used for what purpose?
   a. To measure abstract traits
   b. To predict future behavior
   c. To determine the ability to master skills or knowledge
   d. To compare test scores

9. Which theorist developed ideas on fluid and crystallized intelligence?
   a. John Ertl
   b. Alfred Binet
   c. Sir Francis Galton
   d. Raymond Cattell

10. Why did John Ertl invent a neural efficiency analyzer to more effectively measure intelligence?
   a. He believed traditional intelligence tests were limited to understanding an abstract degree of intelligence.
   b. His rival, Robert Williams, was gaining popularity with his own intelligence test, and Ertl wanted one that surpassed Williams' genius.
   c. He had been injured in an intelligence test in the past and wanted to develop an intelligence test that was safe for the subject.
   d. He believed that genetic factors were the most influential indicator of intelligence.

11. The Black Intelligence Test of Cultural Homogeneity, designed by Robert Williams, was used to do what?
   a. Show cultural dissimilarities
   b. Expose cultural bias in testing
   c. Test one's cultural background
   d. All of the above

12. Mrs. Louise favors Judge Benson above all the other judges in Wilmington, North Carolina. Judge Benson is tall, has blue eyes, speaks clearly, and smiles warmly anytime Mrs. Louise walks into the room. What kind of effect does Judge Benson have on Mrs. Louise?
   a. Halo Effect
   b. Bystander Effect
   c. Audience Effect
   d. Bandwagon Effect

13. Fluid Intelligence refers to what type of abilities?
   a. Thinking and acting quickly, solving new problems
   b. Utilizing learned skills
   c. Adapting to new situations
   d. Developing opportunity from adversity

14. Which of the following is known as the standard score?
   a. T-Score
   b. Measure
   c. Z-Score
   d. Q-Sort

15. What kind of test is used to explore the client's unconscious attitudes or motivations?
    a. Objective test
    b. Projective test
    c. Free choice test
    d. Vertical test

Answer Explanations

1. A: Face validity is obvious to any user, so it's considered common sense. It also doesn't require verification by a professional, like curricular validity does, which makes Choice *B* incorrect. Choice *C* is closer to criterion validity, which measures success and the relationship between a test score and an outcome. Choice *D* is closer to construct validity, which refers to a test that measures abstract traits or theories, and isn't inadvertently testing another variable.

2. C: The Stanford-Binet Intelligence Scale is an intelligence test. The other three answers, Minnesota Multiphasic Personality Inventory (MMPI-2), Beck Depression Inventory, and Myers-Briggs Inventory (MBTI), are types of personality tests.

3. D: Parallel-Forms Reliability involves administering two different versions of an assessment that measures the same set of skills and then correlates the results. Choice *A*, Internal Consistency, refers to how well a test or assessment measures what it's intended to measure, while producing similar results each time. Choice *B*, Inter-Rater Reliability, checks to see that raters do so in agreement, and prevents overly subjective ratings. Choice *C*, Test-Retest Reliability, involves administering the same test twice to a group of individuals, then correlating the scores to evaluate stability.

4. C: Achievement tests measure learning and are often given at the end of grade levels. Aptitude tests measure potential, making Choice *A* incorrect. Personality tests measure unconscious behaviors, making Choice *B* incorrect. Intelligence tests measure intellectual capacity, making Choice *D* incorrect.

5. B: Isabella's friend is probably referring to an occupational test. Occupational tests assess skills or interests as they relate to occupational choices. Intelligence tests, Choice *A*, measure mental capability and potential, so this test is irrelevant for Isabella's current purposes. Achievement tests, Choice *C*, measure knowledge of a specific subject and are primarily only used in education, so this choice is incorrect. Personality tests, Choice *D*, help the test-taker understand personality traits and underlying behaviors, so this is also irrelevant in this situation.

6. C: Alfred Binet created one of the first intelligence tests which, when brought to the U.S., became the Stanford-Binet. Sir Francis Galton and Raymond Cattell, Choices *A* and *D*, studied intelligence, but didn't create the first tests. Choice *B*, Carl Jung, inspired personality tests with his theories, but he never created a way to measure intelligence by a structured test.

7. A: Choice *A* is incorrect; this violates counselor/client confidentiality laws. Ensuring the client's needs are within the counselor's scope of practice, helping the client gain a better understanding of themselves, and evaluating the effectiveness of counseling interventions are all reasons a counselor would administer a test to a client.

8. B: Predictive validity predicts behavior in the future. Abstract traits, Choice *A*, are measured via construct validity. The ability to master skills, Choice *C*, is done through aptitude testing. Concurrent validity compares test results, Choice *D*.

9. D: Raymond Cattell proposed the concept of fluid and crystallized intelligence in the 1940s. John Ertl, Choice *A*, invented a neural efficiency analyzer that measured the speed and efficiency of electrical activity in the brain using an EEG. Alfred Binet, Choice *B*, developed the first test to determine which children would succeed in school. Sir Francis Galton, Choice *C*, believed that intelligence was genetically determined and could be promoted through selective parenting.

10. A: He believed traditional intelligence tests were limited to understanding an abstract degree of intelligence. Choices *B* and *C* are incorrect; Robert Williams did invent an intelligence test, but Ertl did not invent his test to compete with Williams. Also, Ertl was not injured in an intelligence test in the past, so this choice is also incorrect. Choice *D* is incorrect; Arthur Jensen believed that genetic factors were the most influential indicator of intelligence, and this idea has nothing to do with inventing a neural efficiency analyzer.

11. D: All of the above. The Black Intelligence Test of Cultural Homogeneity (B.I.T.C.H. Test) was a culture-specific test designed to expose cultural and racial bias in testing and to prove the dissimilarities of cultures within the U.S.

12. A: The Halo Effect is a type of cognitive bias in which positive perceptions of an individual influence views. Mrs. Louise has a positive perception of Judge Benson due to his attractive appearance, and she is mistakenly extending that attractiveness to his personality. Choice *B*, the bystander effect, occurs when a crowd of people witness a traumatic event and no one steps up to help because they think the next person in the crowd is likely to help. Choice *C*, the audience effect, is when people perform differently in the presence of other people than when alone. Choice *D*, the bandwagon effect, is when a person does something merely because the rest of the group are doing it despite what their own beliefs are about the action.

13. A: Fluid intelligence refers to the ability to think and act quickly and solve new problems. It is independent of education and culture, making the other choices incorrect.

14. C: A Z-score, which measures how many standard deviations from the mean a raw score is, can also be called a standard score. Therefore, Choice *C* is correct.

15. B: A projective test would be given to explore the client's unconscious attitudes or motivations. An objective test, Choice *A*, gives questions with clear correct or incorrect answers and is not open to interpretation. A free choice test, Choice *C*, allows for an open-ended response, but this is a much more general answer choice than Choice *B*, making it incorrect. A vertical test, Choice *D*, is a same-subject test given to different levels or ages, which is incorrect.

Research and Program Evaluation

This section covers the following: research methods, an overview of statistics and statistical methods, ethical considerations in research, and the legal considerations of research. Important terms can be found in the glossary that follows this section.

Research

Simply defined, research means to systematically investigate an experience either to understand what causes it, or to develop a theory about how that experience can cause a future event. Systematic investigation can occur through a number of different scientific methods. Deductive research focuses on a specific theory, and then establishes hypotheses to methodically test the theory in order to support or discredit it. Deductive research often involves setting up experiments, trials, or data collection surveys to collect information related to the theory. Inductive research examines information that's already available (such as established datasets like the U.S. Census Report) to highlight data trends and make inferences and/or projections from those patterns. Research designs determine how to structure a study based on factors such as variables being tested, the level to which the researcher is manipulating a variable in the study, the types of subjects in the study, what the study is testing or looking for, the frequency and duration of data collection, and whether the data collected is qualitative or quantitative in nature. These concepts will be examined further in the following sections.

Non-Experimental Quantitative Research

Quantitative research utilizes logical, empirical methods of collecting information. This information is called data and is often analyzed using statistics. Non-experimental quantitative research includes forms of data collection where the researcher collects data that's already available in some form. They then analyze this dataset to describe the relationship between pre-determined variables. The researcher does not set up a novel system of trials to produce new data, and they can't randomize any data collected. The researcher has no part in manipulating any variables or establishing a separate control group to which they can compare collected data. The lack of a control group, lack of variable manipulation by the researcher, and lack of randomization are often seen as weaknesses in non-experimental quantitative research studies. Some examples of non-experimental quantitative research designs are depicted below.

Survey Designs
These can be conducted through telephone or face-to-face interviews. They can also be conducted through paper or electronic questionnaires (either at an external facility or at the study participant's home). Survey designs are generally used when research about a particular topic is limited so that more information can be gathered to better shape the research question or topic. Surveys are easy (and usually cost-efficient) to administer, but they can also result in low or biased participant response rates.

Correlational Designs
These analyze the strength of the relationship between two variables in one group. One unique type of correlational design is found in ex post facto studies. The researcher examines two existing groups and analyzes the correlation between the variables of interest. Another unique type of correlational design is found in prediction studies, where the researcher determines a correlation between variables, and then uses it to predict other correlations, related events, or future events. The strength and description of the correlation is indicated by the correlation coefficient (r), which falls between -1 and 1. If r = 0, it

indicates there's no relationship between the two variables, while r = 1 indicates a direct, perfect correlation. If *r* equals a negative value, it indicates an inverse relationship between the two variables. If *r* equals a positive value, it indicates a direct relationship between the two variables. Regardless of how strong the correlation is between two variables, it doesn't indicate that one causes the other. It simply indicates that these two variables tend to occur (or not occur) together to some degree.

Comparative Designs
These examine data trends to determine a relationship in two groups or datasets that have already been established.

Qualitative Research

Qualitative research is commonly employed in social sciences, including the field of counseling. It typically focuses on the analysis of a group of people (which is sometimes biased) to understand different aspects of human behavior, relationships, and social interactions. The researcher does not manipulate variables when conducting qualitative research. Qualitative research is primarily conducted without rigid structures in place. Data is collected through the following:

Case Studies
These are detailed and documented examples of the topic of interest. They can be real or hypothetical situations. Case studies often record data over a period of time to examine a specific variable of interest. They can examine a situation involving one individual, a family, a larger community of people, or an organization. Case studies frequently look at how people relate to one another, and/or to their physical or emotional environment.

Focus Groups
These bring together a relatively small group of individuals. The group can be diverse in nature or have many similar interests. A facilitator guides a discussion within the group to discern information about individual or collective viewpoints about a specific issue.

Interviews
These are typically more personal in nature. Interviews can be conducted in person, over the telephone, or via e-mail or regular mail. The interviewer asks the individual or group a series of meaningful questions related to the research topic. The interview can be structured with the interviewer having pre-set questions to ask, or it can be unstructured with the interviewer asking questions based on the flow of conversation and the answers given by the interviewee(s).

Observation
In an observation, the researcher simply watches the individual or group of interest. However, a number of additional factors usually shapes the development of the observation study. The researcher can observe the participant(s) in a specific situation or highly controlled context, or the researcher can observe the participant(s) in their day-to-day routine. The participant(s) may or may not know that they are being observed for specific behaviors. The researcher can involve themselves in the context and become part of the observation study. The researcher can also freely write down data from the observations, or use a pre-made scale or data sheet to document specific behaviors.

Experimental and Quasi-Experimental Quantitative Research

Experimental quantitative research employs highly controlled processes with the hope of determining a causal relationship between one or more input (independent) variables and one or more outcome (dependent) variables. It uses random sampling and assignment methods to make inferences for larger populations. Typically, it compares a control group (serving as a baseline) to a test group. Ideally, experimental studies or experiments should be able to be replicated numerous times with the same results. The ultimate goal of a well-designed experiment is to declare that a particular variable is responsible for a particular outcome, and that, without that variable, the associated outcome wouldn't occur.

Quasi-experimental quantitative research employs many of these same qualities, but it often doesn't use random sampling or assignment in its studies or experiments. Consequently, quasi-experimental research produces results that often don't apply to the population at large. They do, however, often provide meaningful results for certain subgroups of the population.

External Validity

External validity illustrates how well inferences from a sample set can predict similar inferences in a larger population (i.e., can results in a controlled lab setting hold true when replicated in the real world). A sample set with strong external validity allows the researcher to generalize or, in other words, to make strongly supported assumptions about a larger group. For a sample to have strong external validity, it needs to have similar characteristics and context to the larger population about which the researcher is hoping to make inferences. A researcher typically wants to generalize three areas:

- Population: Can inferences from the sample set hold true to a larger group of people, beyond the specific people in the sample?
- Environment: Can inferences from the sample set hold true in settings beyond the specific one used in the study?
- Time: Can inferences from the sample set hold true in any season or temporal period?

If results from the sample set can't hold true across these three areas, the external validity of the study is considered threatened or weak. External validity is strengthened by the number of study replications the researcher is able to successfully complete for multiple settings, groups, and contexts. External validity can also be strengthened by ensuring the sample set is as randomized as possible.

Internal Validity

Internal validity illustrates the integrity of the results obtained from a sample set, and indicates how reliably a specific study or intervention was conducted. Strong internal validity allows the researcher to confidently link a specific variable or process of the study to the results or outcomes. The strength of a study's internal validity can be threatened by the presence of many independent variables. This can result in confounding, where it's difficult to pinpoint exactly what is causing the changes in the dependent variables. The internal validity can also be threatened by biases (sampling bias, researcher bias, or participant bias) as well as historical, personal, and/or contextual influences outside the researcher's control (natural disasters, political unrest, participant death, or relocation). Internal validity can be strengthened by designing highly controlled study or experiment settings that limit these threats.

Sampling

Sampling is the method of collecting participants for a study. It's a crucial component of the research design and study process. There are a number of different ways to select samples, and each method has pros, cons, and situations where it's the most appropriate one to use.

Simple Random Sampling

For this type of probability sampling, the participants are taken directly from a larger population with the characteristics of interest. Each individual in the larger population has the same chance of being selected for the sample.

- Pros: closely represents the target population, thus allowing for results that are the highest in validity
- Cons: obtaining the sample can be time consuming
- Use When: a highly controlled experiment setting is necessary

Stratified Random Sampling

For this type of probability sampling, the researchers first examine the traits of the larger population, which are often demographic or social traits like age, education status, marital status, and household income. They then divide the population into groups (or strata) based on these traits. Members of the population are only included in one stratum. Researchers then randomly sample across each stratum to create the final sample set for the study.

- Pros: closely represents the target population, which allows for results that are highest in validity. Since the sampling method is so specific, researchers are able to use smaller samples.

- Cons: obtaining the sample can be tedious. Researchers may first need to compile and become acutely knowledgeable about the demographic characteristics of the target population before selecting a representative sample.

- Use When: a highly controlled experiment setting is necessary; demographic, social, and/or economic characteristics of the target population are of special interest in the study; or researchers are studying relationships or interactions between two subsets within the larger population

Systematic Random Sampling

For this type of probability sampling, researchers pick a random integer (n), and then select every nth person from the target population for the research sample.

- Pros: a simple, cost-effective sampling technique that generally provides a random sample for the researchers. It ensures that sampling occurs evenly throughout an entire target population.

- Cons: researchers need to ensure that their original target population (from which the sample is selected) is randomized and that every individual has an equal probability of being selected. Researchers need to be familiar with the demographics of the target population to ensure that certain trends don't appear across the selected participants and skew the results.

- Use When: a highly controlled experiment setting is necessary; researchers are short on time or funding and need a quick, cost-efficient method to create a random sample

Convenience Sampling

This is a type of non-probability sampling where researchers select participants who are easily accessible due to factors like location, expense, or volunteer recruitment.

- Pros: saves time and is cost-effective since researchers can create their sample based on what permits the easiest and fastest recruiting of participants

- Cons: highly prone to bias. Is difficult to generalize the results for the population at large since the sample selection is not random.

- Use When: conducting initial trials of a new study, when researchers are simply looking for basic information about the larger population (i.e., to create a more detailed hypothesis for future research)

Ad Hoc Sample

For this type of non-probability sampling, researchers must meet a set quota for a certain characteristic and can recruit any participant as long as they have the desired characteristics.

- Pros: allows for greater inclusion of a population that might not otherwise be represented
- Cons: results won't be indicative of the actual population in an area
- Use When: it's necessary that a group within the larger population needs a set level of representation within the study

Purposive Sampling

Another non-probability sampling method used when researchers have a precise purpose or target population in mind.

- Pros: helps increase recruitment numbers in otherwise hard-to-access populations
- Cons: usually unable to generalize the results to larger populations beyond the sample's specific subset
- Use When: researchers have a precise purpose for the study, or a specific group of participants is required that isn't easy to select through probability sampling methods

Levels of Measurement

Levels of measurement describe the type of data collected during a study or experiment.

- Nominal: This measurement describes variables that are categories (e.g., gender, dominant hand, height).

- Ordinal: This measurement describes variables that can be ranked (e.g., Likert scales, 1 to 10 rating scales).

- Interval: This measurement describes variables that use equally spaced intervals (e.g., number of minutes, temperature).

- Ratio: This measurement describes anything that has a true "zero" point available (e.g., angles, dollars, cents).

Independent and Dependent Variables and Type I and Type II Errors

A variable is one factor in a study or experiment. An independent variable is controlled by the researcher and usually influences the dependent variable (the factor that's typically measured and recorded by the researcher).

In experiments, the researcher declares a hypothesis that a relationship doesn't exist between two variables, groups, or tangible instances. This hypothesis is referred to as the null hypothesis. Errors can be made in accepting or rejecting the null hypothesis based on the outcomes of the experiment. If the researcher rejects the null hypothesis when it's actually true, this is known as a type I error. A type I error indicates that a relationship between two variable exists when, in reality, it doesn't. If the researcher fails to reject the null hypothesis when it's actually false, this is known as a type II error. A type II error indicates that a relationship between two variables doesn't exist when, in reality, it does. These errors typically result when the experiment or study has weak internal validity.

T-Test

A t-test is a statistical testing method used to determine the probability that, when comparing two separate sample sets with different means, the difference in the means is statistically significant. In other words, researchers can infer that the same difference will be found between the same two groups in the target population as opposed to only being found between the two specific sample sets. Usually the t-test is only used when the data sets have normal distributions and low standard deviations. The calculated t-test statistic corresponds to a table of probability values. These values indicate the likelihood that the difference between groups is simply due to chance. Traditionally, if the t-test statistic corresponds with less than a 5 percent probability that the differences between the two data sets are by chance, then researchers can assume that there's a statistically significant difference between the two sample sets.

Forms of Hypothesis

A hypothesis typically takes one of two forms:

- Null Hypothesis: declares there is no relationship between two variables
- Alternative Hypothesis: declares a specific relationship between two variables, or simply states that the null hypothesis is rejected

Analyses of Variance

Variance tests examine the means of two or more sample sets to detect statistically significant differences in the samples. Analyses of variance tests (commonly referred to as ANOVA tests) are more efficient and accurate than t-tests when there are more than two sample sets. There are multiple types of ANOVA tests. One-way ANOVA tests are used when there's only one factor of influence across the sample sets. Consequently, two- and three-way ANOVA tests exist and are used in the case of additional factors. ANOVA tests can also analyze differences in sample sets where there are multiple dependent and independent variables. ANOVA tests work by creating ratios of variances between and within the sample sets to determine whether the differences are statistically significant. Calculating these ratios is fairly tedious, and researchers generally use statistical software packages such as SPSS, SAS, or Minitab to input the data sets and run the calculations. SPSS stands for Statistical Package for the Social Science and is one of the most popular packages that performs complex data manipulation with easy

instructions. SAS stands for Statistical Analysis System, and is a software developed for advanced analytics, data management, business intelligence, multivariate analyses, and predictive analytics. Minitab is an all-purpose statistical software created for simple interactive use.

Analyses of Covariance

This analysis is a type of ANOVA. This analysis is used to control for potential confounding variables, and is commonly referred to as ANCOVA. Say a researcher is testing the effect of classical music on elementary students' ability to solve math problems. If the students being tested are in varying grades, then their grade level must be taken into account. This is because math ability generally increases with grade level. ANCOVA provides a way to measure and remove the skewing effects of grade level in order to better understand the correlation that's being tested.

Chi-Square and Bivariate Tabular Analysis

Similar to statistical testing methods like t-tests and ANOVA tests, a chi-square test analyzes data between independent groups. However, chi-square tests focus on variables that have categorical data rather than numerical data. They can only be run on data with whole integer tallies or counts, and they're typically used when a researcher has large, normally distributed, and unpaired sample sets.

Bivariate tabular analysis is a basic form of analysis used when the value of an independent variable is known to predict an exact value for the dependent variable. This is most commonly illustrated by a traditional XY plot graph that marks independent variable (X) values across the horizontal access, and marks dependent variable (Y) values along the vertical access. Once all of the values are plotted, a relationship (or lack thereof) can be seen between the independent and dependent variable.

Post Hoc and Nonparametric Tests

Post hoc tests are usually performed after running other tests (e.g., t-tests or ANOVA tests) where it's been determined that statistically significant differences exist between two or more sample sets. At this point, researchers can pick and choose specific groups between which to analyze similarities or differences. Some common post hoc tests are the Least Significant Difference test, Tukey's test, and confidence interval tests, which are often similar to running multiple t-tests. Post hoc tests can be complex and time-consuming to calculate by hand or with simple software, so they often must be completed using sophisticated statistical software packages.

Nonparametric tests are typically used when datasets don't have pre-set parameters, are skewed in distribution, include outliers, or are unconventional in some other way. As a result, nonparametric tests are less likely to be valid in showing strong relationships, similarities, or when differences between groups exist. It's also easier to make a type I error when running nonparametric tests. Some common nonparametric tests include the Mood's Median test, the Kruskal-Wallis test, and the Mann-Whitney test.

Accountability

Accountability is an important aspect in conducting research. Researchers typically need to have a purpose for conducting their studies. This purpose should be beneficial to the target population, fair, timely, cost-efficient, and should not harm any groups in the process. Funding sources, as well as internal and external auditing groups, may regularly evaluate research operations and outcomes. This is done to ensure that the funds are used appropriately, the research process is ethical, and useful results

are obtained. Typically, structured evaluation processes (such as benchmarks and reporting practices) are established and documented during the study's planning and proposal periods.

Writing Issues Faced in Doing Research

When writing research proposals, reports, or manuscripts, researchers may run into issues. These can include inefficient time and project management, incorrect or missing source citations, or failure to acknowledge personnel on final document submissions. When submitting final documents, researchers should be aware of any stylistic, formatting, or content guidelines, as these can vary by agency and publication. It's considered good practice and standard convention not to submit the same manuscript to multiple publications since it's disrespectful to the editors' time. It also increases the possibility that the manuscript could be published more than once, which could mislead other researchers who may be citing that study. Even with hard work and due diligence, researchers should be prepared to have final manuscripts returned or rejected. Manuscripts sometimes even require multiple rounds of revisions before the publishing body determines that they're ready for publication.

Ethical Issues Faced in Doing Research

Researchers should strive not to harm any population when conducting studies or experiments. All biomedical and behavioral research requires the approval of an independent institutional review board (IRB) to begin. In addition, the IRB monitors the research study for its duration to ensure that populations aren't experiencing any harm. Typically, IRB-approved studies require a participant consent form, the guarantee of anonymity and/or confidentiality for all participants and associated data, and strict monitoring and evaluation processes.

Researchers should also be mindful of producing, collecting, and publishing accurate, authentic, and non-biased data. Failure to collect or publish data that does not support the researchers' hypotheses or motives—or that inadvertently brings awareness to another sensitive issue—can also be grounds for ethical concern.

Education Resources Information Center (ERIC)

The Education Resources Information Center (ERIC) is a scholarly online database funded by the United States Department of Education. It contains over 1.5 million pieces of high-level, educational literature dating back to 1966.

Important Terms

Confounding: an effect that occurs in an experiment or study due to the presence of an extra variable that can influence or correlate with the established independent or dependent variables

Control Group: in an experiment or study, this group mirrors the qualities of the test group as much as possible, but does not receive the test or intervention in order to serve as a comparison

Correlation: the relationship or degree of interaction between two variables

Correlation Coefficient: a value between -1.0 and 1.0 that illustrates the strength of a relationship or interaction between two variables, with zero indicating no relationship

Dependent Variable: in an experiment or study, the variable that changes due to manipulation of the independent variable

Empirical: based on observation, experience, and/or experimentation

Hypothesis: a prediction made in order to lay the foundation for ensuing tests, experiments, or empirical data collection and analysis

Mean: the central value of a data distribution

Non-Probability Sampling: sampling method that doesn't choose sample sets at random

Observation: watching and documenting an experience in detail

Probability Sampling: sampling method that chooses sample sets at random; generally more likely to represent the target population

Qualitative: focusing on the qualities and/or descriptors of a phenomenon

Quantitative: focusing on the numerical, mathematical, statistical, or otherwise quantifiable aspects of a phenomenon

Regression Analysis: a statistical technique to determine interactions and relationships between variables, usually to make predictions

Statistically Significant: the probability of a relationship, result, or event occurring due to something other than chance

Theory: a widely accepted principle or set of ideas that explain an event or events (though a theory can be disproven)

Variable: a factor that can be changed

Practice Questions

1. Case studies, focus groups, and research observation are all examples of what kind of data collection methods?
   a. Qualitative data collection methods
   b. Quantitative data collection methods
   c. Purposive sampling
   d. Systematic random sampling

2. Quasi-experimental research methods follow most processes associated with experimental research methods except for _____; therefore, any results obtained usually cannot be _____.
   a. Data synthesis; analyzed
   b. Trial and error practices; used
   c. Randomization; generalized
   d. Clinical trial studies; medical

3. Which visual representation is most often used to present bivariate tabular analyses?
   a. Parabola
   b. Pie chart
   c. Cross-sectional 2 x 2 table
   d. XY graph

4. Which of the following is true given the advent of technology in the counseling field?
   a. Technology has advanced the counseling field because it eliminates geographical barriers and can be less tedious to document cases.
   b. Technology has devastated the counseling field by making counseling sessions more robotic and by lacking the personal touch of an in-person session.
   c. Currently, there is not sufficient evidence as to whether or not technology is advantageous or disadvantageous to the counseling field.
   d. Technology is seen as a necessity to the counseling field, as it allows easier access to clients.

5. A study is considered to have strong external validity if the researcher can replicate and generalize its findings across multiple instances of what three factors?
   a. Population, time, and environment
   b. Gender, age, and height
   c. Animal studies, human studies, and non-living object studies
   d. Infant years, adolescent years, and adult years

6. Bill is conducting a research study on workplace views of maternity leave in a specific industry. His funding source requires that at least 60 percent of his sample set be women. The industry that he's studying consists of 32 percent women, and he has to search a little harder to find enough female participants. This is an example of what type of sampling?
   a. Simple random sampling
   b. Stratified random sampling
   c. Ad hoc sampling
   d. Systematic random sampling

7. Tina is conducting a research study about underage drinking habits on college campuses on football game days. As she's scoring her collected data, she notices the test group is primarily made up of freshman students and the control group is primarily made up of sophomore students. What does Tina realize about this distinction?
   a. It's to be expected
   b. It may confound her results
   c. It won't make a difference if she runs enough ANOVA tests
   d. It should be tabulated in a chi-square cross section

8. A physician administers a new pain medication as part of a clinical trial, and later asks the participants to rank their pain on a scale of one to five. The patients' responses are an example of what type of measure?
   a. Interval
   b. Nominal
   c. Ordinal
   d. Ratio

9. Nonparametric tests are more likely to result in which of the following?
   a. Type I error
   b. Type II error
   c. Confounding
   d. Independent variables

10. Rachel is going out for lunch. As she leaves her office, she wonders if eating veggie tacos for lunch has any effect on how many data sets someone can analyze in a given afternoon. When she returns from lunch, she conducts a literature review to see what data is available on this topic. She finds none. Over the next few weeks, when any of her colleagues leave for the day at the same time as she does, Rachel asks them what they ate for lunch and how many data sets they analyzed after 1:00 pm. The type of sample Rachel is collecting is referred to as which of the following?
   a. Simple random sample
   b. Convenience sample
   c. Systematic sample
   d. Stratified random sample

11. Julia is collecting a stratified random sample to see if the level of education correlates with household income in the state of Texas. If 28 percent of the people in Texas have at least a bachelor's degree, what percentage of Julia's sample set needs to have a bachelor's degree?
   a. 28 percent
   b. 50 percent
   c. 78 percent
   d. 90 percent

12. Joanna is interested in the attitudes, beliefs, and perceptions of working fathers toward the quality and affordability of childcare. She books a conference room in her office, invites fifteen fathers working in her building to attend a two-hour session, and presents them with a series of questions to discuss with each other. They can also direct any questions and comments about the topic to Joanna. She mainly documents the conversation but, if there's a lull in the conversation, she joins in to facilitate the discussion. This is an example of conducting which of the following?

    a. Case study
    b. Survey
    c. Focus group
    d. Observation

13. One fundamental difference between probability sampling and non-probability sampling is that probability sampling uses _____ while non-probability sampling does not.

    a. Convenience
    b. Randomization
    c. Volunteerism
    d. Referral

14. The correlation coefficient value falls between which values?

    a. Zero and 100
    b. -5 and 5
    c. Zero and 1
    d. -1 and 1

15. A researcher is grouping participants into sample sets by gender. In this instance, gender is an example of what type of measure?

    a. Interval
    b. Nominal
    c. Ordinal
    d. Ratio

16. Joe is doing a research study on the effects alcohol consumption has on long-term mood. His control sample self-reports not drinking any alcohol. His test sample self-reports drinking at least one glass of wine every night. He collects self-reported data on each group's mood for sixty days. Both data sets have normal distribution and low standard deviation. Joe now wants to test the statistical significance of the difference in mood between the control group and the test group. Which test should Joe conduct?

    a. T-test
    b. Chi-square test
    c. ANOVA test
    d. Post hoc test

17. The acronym ERIC stands for what?

    a. Electronic Research Institute Collaboration
    b. Education Resources Information Center
    c. Education Research Information Center
    d. Electronic Research Incorporated

18. Who funds ERIC?
    a. A committee of universities and colleges from across the United States
    b. Google
    c. The United States Department of Education
    d. The United States Congress

19. Which of the following is a popular statistical software program?
    a. SPSS
    b. SAS
    c. Minitab
    d. All of the above

20. A researcher notes changes in the outdoor temperature over a one-month period. The recorded temperatures are an example of what type of measure?
    a. Interval
    b. Nominal
    c. Ordinal
    d. Ratio

21. A type II error _____ a _____ null hypothesis.
    a. Rejects; true
    b. Rejects; false
    c. Fails to reject; true
    d. Fails to reject; false

22. Anna is doing a research study on the effect various study habits have on test scores. She collects four sample sets from a Psychology 101 class of four hundred students and has each group practice a different habit while studying for the first exam. The first sample group listens to classical music during every study session. The second sample group exercises for thirty minutes before every study session. The third sample group naps after every study session. The fourth sample group drinks coffee before every study session. Anna collects exam scores for every participant and wants to test the statistical significance of the differences between scores for the sample groups. Anna should conduct which of the following tests?
    a. T-test
    b. Chi-square test
    c. ANOVA test
    d. Post hoc test

23. All biomedical and behavioral research proposals require approval by whom?
    a. A government employee
    b. A six-person committee of licensed research physicians (typically those in the field of the research topic) and/or psychologists
    c. An institutional review board
    d. A participant from the sample group

24. It is good practice and standard convention to submit final manuscripts for scholarly publication to how many journal(s) or publisher(s)?

    a. One
    b. Two
    c. Three
    d. Four

25. A type I error _____ a _____ null hypothesis.

    a. Rejects; true
    b. Rejects; false
    c. Fails to reject; true
    d. Fails to reject; false

26. A researcher is analyzing trends in insurance reimbursement for counseling costs from 1990 to 2010. The changes in reimbursement are an example of what type of measure?

    a. Interval
    b. Nominal
    c. Ordinal
    d. Ratio

Answer Explanations

1. A: Case studies, focus groups, and research observation are all examples of qualitative data collection methods. These methods collect data related to descriptors and details, rather than data related to counts and numbers. Quantitative data collection focuses on the numerical mathematical, statistical, or otherwise quantifiable aspects of a phenomenon, making Choice *B* incorrect. Purposive sampling, Choice *C*, are non-probability sampling methods used when researchers have a precise purpose or target population in mind. In systematic random sampling, Choice *D*, researchers pick a random integer (n), and then select every *n*th person from the target population for the research sample.

2. C: Randomization; generalized. Though quasi-experimental research methods usually don't produce results that can be applied to larger populations, they often produce results that can apply to specific subsets of populations.

3. D: An XY graph is most often used to present bivariate tabular analyses. Bivariate tabular analyses are typically depicted this way since they calculate data points representing independent variables (plotted on the horizontal X-axis) to predict data points representing dependent variables (plotted on the vertical Y-axis).

4. C: Currently, there is not sufficient evidence as to whether or not technology is advantageous or disadvantageous to the counseling field. Choice *A* is incorrect because it provides an opinion—that technology has advanced the counseling field—as a fact. Choice *B* is incorrect for the same reason as Choice *A*; there is no evidence yet of technology being advantageous or disadvantageous to the counseling field. Choice *D* is close; "Technology is seen as a necessity" might be partially true for some people. However, this is not the best possible answer, as it does not contain the whole truth, so it is incorrect.

5. A: Population, time and environment. If a research design can produce the same outcomes across multiple types of people, multiple seasons or temporal periods, and across a variety of settings and situational contexts, it is considered to have high external validity. Any results are likely generalizable to the target population.

6. C: In ad hoc sampling, the sampling cannot be randomized if the researcher needs to meet a certain quota for whatever reason. This makes it easier to get the necessary participants, but will lower generalizability to the target population. For Choice *A*, simple random sampling, the participants are taken directly from a larger population with the characteristics of interest. Each individual in the larger population has the same chance of being selected for the sample. For Choice *B*, stratified random sampling, researchers first examine the traits of the larger population, then divide the population into groups based on these traits. Members of the population are only included in one stratum. Researchers then randomly sample across each stratum to create the final sample set for the study. In Choice *D*, systematic random sampling, researchers pick a random integer (n), and then select every *n*th person from the target population for the research sample.

7. B: Tina realizes that this distinction may confound her results. Confounding occurs when any results found correlate with multiple variables, therefore preventing a clear correlation between a particular independent variable and a particular dependent variable. In this instance, the fact that a majority of the test group and control group are each made up of a particular year of students may influence the presence of any habits that Tina is trying to study.

8. C: The patients' responses are an example of an ordinal measure. An ordinal measure describes variables that fall on a scale or can be ranked. An interval measure, Choice *A*, describes variables that use equally spaced intervals (e.g., number of minutes, temperature). A nominal measure, Choice *B*, describes variables that are categorical in nature. A ratio measure, Choice *D*, describes anything that has a true "zero" point available (e.g., angles, dollars, cents).

9. A: Type I error. Since nonparametric tests work with data sets that tend to be noisy in some way (outliers, abnormal distribution, et cetera), they may show an effect between variables when there isn't actually one. Choice *B*, a type II error, indicates that a relationship between two variables doesn't exist when, in reality, it does. Choice *C*, confounding, is an effect that occurs in an experiment or study due to the presence of an extra variable that can influence or correlate with the established independent or dependent variables, making this answer incorrect. Choice *D* is incorrect. Tests usually do not result in independent variables. Independent variables are variables that stand alone and are not changed by other variables attempting to be measured.

10. B: The type of sample Rachel is collecting is referred to as a convenience sample. Rachel is collecting information from people who work with her and who she sees at a good time, so she is collecting samples based on proximity. This sample is not indicative of the general population and can be biased, but it could provide Rachel with enough information to create a detailed hypothesis for more rigorous testing in the future. Choice *A*, simple random sample, participants are taken directly from a larger population with the characteristics of interest. Each individual in the larger population has the same chance of being selected for the sample, so this choice is incorrect. In Choice *C*, systematic sampling, researchers pick a random integer (*n*), and then select every *n*th person from the target population for the research sample, so this is also incorrect. In Choice *D*, stratified random sampling, researchers first examine the traits of the larger population, then divide the population into groups based on these traits, so this is also incorrect.

11. A: 28 percent of Julia's sample set needs to have a bachelor's degree. When collecting a stratified random sample, the characteristics of the sample set must exactly match the characteristics of the targeted general population.

12. C: A focus group hopes to facilitate discussion of a particular topic between persons of interest, and the researcher typically collects relevant notes from this discussion. Case studies, Choice *A*, often record data over a period of time to examine a specific variable of interest, so this choice is incorrect. Surveys, Choice *B*, are a method of gathering information from people by telephone, face-to-face interviews, or paper or electronic questionnaires. In an observation, Choice *D*, the researcher simply watches the individual or group of interest and does not participate in the discussion, so this choice is incorrect.

13. B: Probability sampling uses randomization. In probability sampling, anyone who is eligible to be in the sample has an equal chance of getting randomly selected, whereas non-probability sampling may choose participants based on convenience, referral, volunteerism, etc., making Choices *A*, *C*, and *D* incorrect.

14. D: -1 and 1. The correlation coefficient value is always between these two numbers, with zero representing no correlation. A negative value indicates an inverse correlation, and a positive value indicates a direct correlation.

15. B: In this case, gender is an example of a nominal measure. A nominal measure describes variables that are categorical in nature. An interval measure, Choice *A*, describes variables that use equally spaced intervals (e.g., number of minutes, temperature). An ordinal measure, Choice *C*, describes variables that can be ranked (e.g., Likert scales, 1 to 10 rating scales). A ratio measure, Choice D, describes anything that has a true "zero" point available (e.g., angles, dollars, cents).

16. A: Joe should conduct a t-test. A t-test examines differences between two (and only two) normally distributed groups with low standard deviation to determine if the differences are statistically significant or due to chance. Choice B, chi-square tests, can only be run on data with whole integer tallies or counts, and they're typically used when a researcher has large, normally distributed, and unpaired sample sets, so this is incorrect. Choice C is incorrect; ANOVA tests usually test for statistically significant differences between three or more sample sets. A post-hoc test, Choice D, is usually performed after running other tests (e.g., t-tests or ANOVA tests) where it's been determined that statistically significant differences exist between two or more sample sets, so this choice is incorrect.

17. B: ERIC stands for Education Resources Information Center. ERIC is a scholarly online database funded by the United States Department of Education and contains over 1.5 million pieces of high-level, educational literature dating back to 1966.

18. C: The United States Department of Education funds ERIC. The DOE has been sponsoring ERIC since the 1960s.

19. D: All of the above. SPSS, SAS, and Minitab are all popular statistical software programs. These programs make it easier to analyze and run tests on large datasets. Choice A, SPSS, stands for Statistical Package for the Social Science and is one of the most popular packages that performs complex data manipulation with easy instructions. Choice B, SAS, stands for Statistical Analysis System, and is a software developed for advanced analytics, data management, business intelligence, multivariate analyses, and predictive analytics. Choice C, Minitab, is an all-purpose statistical software created for simple interactive use.

20. A: The recorded temperatures are an example of an interval measure. An interval measure describes variables that fall at equally spaced intervals. A nominal measure, Choice B, describes variables that are categorical in nature. An ordinal measure, Choice C, describes variables that can be ranked (e.g., Likert scales, 1 to 10 rating scales). A ratio measure, Choice D, describes anything that has a true "zero" point available (e.g., angles, dollars, cents).

21. D: Fails to reject; false. A type II error in statistical testing occurs when the researcher fails to reject a null hypothesis that is false. This type of error in a test will indicate that there is no relationship between two variables when there actually is.

22. C: Anna should conduct an ANOVA test. An analysis of variance (ANOVA) test is the most efficient and most accurate way to test for statistically significant differences between three or more sample sets. Choice A is incorrect, because ANOVA tests are usually more efficient and accurate than t-tests when there are more than two sample sets. Choice B, a chi-square test, focuses on variables that have categorical data rather than numerical data, so this is incorrect. A post-hoc test, Choice D, is usually performed after running other tests (e.g., t-tests or ANOVA tests) where it's been determined that statistically significant differences exist between two or more sample sets, so this choice is also incorrect.

23. C: Biomedical and behavioral research proposals require approval by an institutional review board. An institutional review board is typically an independent committee focused on the ethics of the researched proposal. This board approves the initial proposal, then monitors the project for its duration to ensure no harm comes to research subjects.

24. A: It is good practice to submit final manuscripts for scholarly publication to one journal or publisher. It is important to respect the journal and its editors' time, and to prevent the possibility that original research may be published more than once. This can cause major reference and citation errors for future researchers, especially those conducting meta-analyses.

25. A: Rejects; true. A type I error in statistical testing occurs when the researcher rejects a null hypothesis that is, in fact, true. This type of error in a test will indicate that a relationship occurs between two variables when it actually doesn't.

26. D: The changes in reimbursement are an example of a ratio measure. A ratio measure describes variables that can have a true zero point (in this case, zero dollars and zero cents). An interval measure, Choice *A*, describes variables that use equally spaced intervals (e.g., number of minutes, temperature). A nominal measure, Choice *B*, describes variables that are categorical in nature. An ordinal measure, Choice *C*, describes variables that can be ranked (e.g., Likert scales, 1 to 10 rating scales).

Professional Counseling Orientation and Ethical Practice

History of Counseling Through the 1950s

The practice of counseling has long existed, but before the 18th century, it typically took the form of advice from older family members and religious leaders. The 18th century brought with it the beginnings of industrialization, and society began to place greater value on rigorous scientific methods to explain the world rather than believing every phenomenon was commanded by a religious source. This influenced how society viewed medical, behavioral, and mental anomalies. Previously, demons or other spiritual influences were commonly believed to be the causes behind behaviors that are now diagnosed as illnesses or disorders (such as addictions, hallucinations, and mood instability). In the 18th and 19th centuries, researchers began to examine these through a more "scientific lens."

The professional field of psychotherapy has its roots in Germany, coming into existence as an offshoot of neurology. In 1879, a German physician and professor named Wilhelm Wundt founded the Institute of Experimental Psychology, which was the first of its kind in the world. Near the end of the 1800s, German neurologist Sigmund Freud theorized that trained personnel could analyze a "troubled" person's subconscious to determine why their patient was exhibiting certain behaviors. As this practice grew, psychiatrists and psychologists began to theorize about the human mind and human behavior. In 1913, the first mental health clinic opened in the United States. The text *Workbook in Vocations* by Proctor, Benefield, and Wrenn increased the popularity of counseling after it was written in 1931.

When World War II started, there was a great demand for matching civilian skillsets to military needs, and counselors played a major role. During the war, American psychologist Carl Rogers published *Counseling and Psychotherapy*, which pioneered the movement of involving psychology patients (which he referred to as *clients*) in their own healing. This became known as client-centered therapy and laid the foundation for important aspects of the counseling profession. When World War II ended, the Veteran's Administration pushed to expand counseling services to help returning servicemen transition back into civilian life and the civilian workforce. The American Personnel and Guidance Association (APGA) was formed in 1952, and would later become today's American Counseling Association (ACA).

History of Counseling from 1960 to the Present

The term *counseling* became more mainstream in the 1960s after the National Defense Education Act was passed, which increased funding for counseling education. Scientific ideas supporting holistic health services (such as humanistic theories) were shaped, and the most renowned psychologists in the field were Abraham Maslow and Carl Rogers. Community mental health centers began to emerge across the nation. During the 1960s, Gilbert Wrenn wrote *The Counselor in a Changing World,* urging counselors to focus less on curing emotional illness and to focus more on developmental efforts of the client. During the Vietnam War, most of the counseling expertise and funding were redirected toward the war effort. The 1970s brought a confusing time for counselors, with many working in diverse social settings without clearly defined industry parameters. In 1983, the ACA launched the National Board for Certified Counselors so that the field could have a recognizable credential. As a result, professional and educational standards were created for the counseling field and, in the early 2000s, states began passing legal counseling licensing standards.

Current and Continuing Trends

Legal counseling licensing standards have influenced current and continuing trends in the profession. However, not all states recognize licensing obtained in other states. This is something that may yet face reform. Additionally, the types of services that are considered counseling have expanded. Counselors can be found in vocational, medical, organizational, school, sports, and life coaching settings. In particular, licensed mental health counselors are largely influencing the field of psychiatry. It's expected that they'll handle more of the behavioral and therapeutic cases in the country, while psychiatrists will focus primarily on cases where the client must utilize psycho-pharmaceuticals to manage their diagnosis. Psychologists have opposed counselor licensure in the past, claiming that counselors and social workers do not have qualification to practice. However, more and more states have agreed to pass state licensure laws, granting counselors their right to practice in the field. Finally, technology has impacted all aspects of living. Online counseling and the leveraging of social media as a counseling tool have greatly influenced the field. However, research does not currently exist on whether technology is helpful or harmful to the profession and its clients.

ICD, PL94-142, and the 1958 National Defense Education Act

The International Classification of Diseases (ICD) is a resource published by the World Health Organization (WHO). It provides a snapshot of health statuses, disease concerns, and other epidemiological data by country and population. It is used for research purposes and to manage available, global health resources. The latest edition (ICD-10) was published in 1994, but revisions are currently underway for the next edition (ICD-11) to be published in 2022.

Public Law 94-142 (PL94-142) is known as the Education for All Handicapped Children Act and, more recently, as the Individuals with Disabilities Education Act (IDEA). Enacted by the United States Department of Education in 1975, it declared that tailored public education is guaranteed for all disabled children.

The 1958 National Defense Education Act was a key initiative for the field of counseling, and provided funding in the form of federal grants and loans to individuals who wanted to pursue a formal counseling education. This act was responsible for expanding school guidance services as well as improving guidance for gifted children.

Principle of Ethical Decision-Making and the Purpose of the ACA Code of Ethics

In general, counselors follow basic ethical guidelines to do no physical or psychological harm to their clients or to society, and to provide fair, honest, and compassionate service to their client and society when making professional decisions. The ACA Code of Ethics exists as a resource to provide clear guidelines for counselors to practice by, and as a resource for counselors to consult when facing an ethical decision that they're unsure of making. This Code supports the mission of the counseling profession as established by the ACA.

Ethical Issues

Ethical issues can present themselves in any field. In counseling, ethical issues often center on the confidentiality and anonymity of clients, client cases, and data collected about the client (especially in group or family settings). However, counselors are obligated to report any instances of abuse, self-harm that could lead to a fatality, or harm to others that could lead to fatalities. Counselors also need to ensure that clear personal and professional boundaries are maintained between themselves and their client. In all instances of counseling, practitioners must exhibit respect and tolerance for individuals of all backgrounds, attitudes, opinions, and beliefs.

ACA Code of Ethics

The foundation of the ACA Code of Ethics is defined by the following six core values:

- Autonomy: freedom to govern one's own choices for the future
- Nonmaleficence: causing the least amount of harm as possible
- Beneficence: promoting health and wellbeing for the good of the individual and society
- Justice: treating each individual with fairness and equality
- Fidelity: displaying trust in professional relationships and maintaining promises
- Veracity: making sure to provide the truth in all situations and contacts

The Code of Ethics is comprised of nine sections that cover ethical guidelines to uphold these core values. These nine sections focus on the following:

The Practitioner-Counselor Relationship

The counselor-client relationship is one that is built primarily on trust. Counselors have the obligation to make sure the confidentiality and privacy rights of their clients are protected, and therefore should protect and maintain any documentation recorded during services. Additionally, clients have rights regarding informed consent. Open communication between the client and counselor is essential; in the beginning of the relationship, the counselor must provide the client with information on all services provided, with sensitivity to cultural and developmental diversity. Counselors should also pay special attention to clients that are incapacitated in their abilities to give consent, and should seek a balance between the client's own capacities and their capacity to give consent to a more capable individual. Finally, with mandated clients, counselors should seek transparency in areas regarding information they share with other professionals.

Confidentiality and Privacy

With trust as the cornerstone of the counselor-client relationship, counselors must ensure the confidentiality and privacy of their clients in regards to respecting client rights through multicultural considerations, disclosure of documentation to appropriate professionals, and speaking to their clients about limitations of privacy. Some exceptions to confidentiality include the potential for serious harm to other individuals, end-of-life decisions, information regarding life-threatening diseases, and court-ordered disclosure. Counselors are encouraged to notify clients when disclosing information when possible, with only the minimal amount of information shared.

Professional Responsibility

Counselors have the obligation to facilitate clear communication when dealing with the public or other professionals. They should practice only within their knowledge of expertise and be careful not to apply or participate in work they are not qualified for. Continuing education is part of the counselor's development as a professional, and the counselor should always be aware of evolving information. It's important for counselors to also monitor their own health and wellness, making sure to refer clients to other competent professionals if they find themselves unable to practice due to health or retirement.

Relationships with Other Professionals

Developing relationships with other professionals is important for counselors in order to provide their clients with the best possible resources. Being part of interdisciplinary teams is one way for counselors to provide the best, well-rounded services to clients. Counselors should always be respectful to other professionals with different approaches, as long as those approaches are grounded in scientific research. It is important for counselors to develop and maintain relationships with other professionals.

Evaluation, Assessment, and Interpretation

In order to effectively plan for a client's treatment, general assessments should be made at the beginning of the counselor-client relationship regarding education, mental health, psychology, and career. Clients have a right to know their results and should be informed of the testing and usage of results prior to assessment. Counselors must take into account the cultural background of clients when diagnosing mental disorders, as culture affects the way clients define their problems. Counselors should take care not to evaluate clients they are counseling and vice versa.

Supervision, Training and Teaching

It is important for counselors to foster appropriate relationships with their supervisees and students. A client's wellbeing is encouraged not only by counselors but everyone the counselor works with. For counselors who are involved in supervising others, continuing education is important in providing the students or trainees with correct information. Any sexual relationship with current supervisees or students is prohibited, as well as any personal relationship that affects the counselor's ability to be objective. Finally, counselors should be proactive in maintaining a diverse faculty and/or a diverse student body.

Research and Publication

When conducting research, counselors must take care to make sure they adhere to federal, state, agency, and institutional policies in dealing with confidentiality. Counselors should keep in mind the rights of their participants and facilitate safe practices during research that do not harm the client's wellbeing. As any objective research, counselors should take care not to exaggerate or manipulate their findings in any way, even if the outcome is unfavorable. Counselors should take care where the identity of participants is concerned. All parties involved in the research of case examples must be notified prior to publication and give consent after reviewing the publication themselves. It's important for researchers to give credit to all contributors in publication.

Distance Counseling, Technology, and Social Media

The field of counseling is evolving to include electronic means of helping clients. Counselors should take into consideration the implications of privacy and confidentiality when treating clients online and take precaution in securing these, notifying the clients of any limitations to privacy. It's important to verify the client's identity when using electronic sources throughout the duration of treatment. In distance counseling, counselors must also be aware of the laws in their own state as well as the client's state.

Resolving Ethical Issues

This section ensures that all counselors act in an ethical and legal manner when dealing with clients and other professionals. It's important for counselors to make known their allegiance to the ACA Code of Ethics and try to resolve ethical issues following this manner. If the conflict cannot be resolved this way, counselors may be obligated to solve the conflict through the appropriate legal and/or government authority.

The ACA keeps an updated copy of their Code of Ethics, as well as other media and interactive resources relating to ethical practices, on their website at www.counseling.org.

Important Terms

Defamation: the act of spreading false information in order to damage an individual's reputation

Encryption: encoding virtual information so that it can only be accessed by the sender and the target audience (important for virtual counseling sessions and record-keeping)

EPPP: Examination of Professional Practice in Psychology

Exceptions to Confidentiality: NBCC code of ethics states that client records are to be kept confidential except in cases preventing clear and imminent danger, or where a government agency order is involved

Gestalt: a school of thought in psychology that an entity should be viewed holistically rather than as many parts making up one object

Harassment: any kind of aggressive or unwanted behavior, speech, or instigation

Humanism: a perspective in psychology that focuses on an individual as a whole, rather than on specific traits or characteristics

Humanistic Perspective: a psychological approach that focuses on the positive aspects of human behavior. A Humanistic Life Outlook is formed by a combination of formal education, observational learning experiences, and diverse interpersonal interactions.

Informed Consent: documented permission (typically written and signed) by a participant to engage in a situation, treatment, or study after learning all possible risks and benefits

NBCC: National Board for Certified Counselors. This is formally known as AACD, or American Association for Counseling and Development.

Privileged Communication: communication between the counselor and the client that is protected as a confidential relationship, often protected by law against a forced disclosure

Professional Disclosure Statements: found in the ACA code of ethics, professional disclosure statements are documents that disclose the status of professionals and how their status affects the limits of confidentiality, services rendered, as well as information about the counseling relationship and what to expect

Psychoanalysis: the process of intervening in mental disorders or diseases by studying aspects of the conscious and subconscious mind

Psychotherapy: the process of healing or intervening in mental disorders or diseases through psychological, cognitive, or "talk" therapies rather than through physiological, pharmaceutical, or other medical therapies

Self-Actualization: fulfilling one's personal potential, drive, or intrinsic feeling of purpose

Sliding Scale Fees: the process of adjusting one's fees based on what the client is able to afford

Tarasoff vs. Board of Regents of the University of California: a case in 1976 that came to the conclusion that it was a professional's duty to warn a client who was in imminent danger

Practice Questions

1. What's the primary setting in which a counselor works?
   a. Medical
   b. School
   c. Vocational
   d. All of the above

2. Which of the psychologists below was a pioneer in humanistic theories?
   a. Wilhelm Wundt
   b. Sigmund Freud
   c. Carl Rogers
   d. Raymond Cattell

3. What entity was responsible for supporting and expanding professional counseling services?
   a. The first mental health clinic in the United States
   b. The United States Department of Veterans Affairs
   c. The United States Army
   d. Carl Rogers' first privately funded organization

4. When working with counseling clients online, one way to maintain the privacy section of the ACA Code of Ethics is to do which of the following?
   a. Encrypt all client intake information, communications, evaluations, and other related records
   b. Use personal servers to store client information
   c. Print all of the client's records and store them in a filing cabinet
   d. Let the client know before you begin treatment that you cannot guarantee any privacy when working virtually

5. "Do no harm" is deemed as a value in the ACA Code of Ethics by what principle?
   a. Nonhomogeneity
   b. Nonmalignant
   c. Nonmaleficence
   d. Nonchalance

6. Which of the following entities publishes the International Classification of Diseases (ICD)?
   a. The World Health Organization
   b. The United Nations
   c. The International Journal of Health Sciences
   d. The United States Agency for International Development

7. In what year did the ACA launch the National Board for Certified Counselors?
   a. 1963
   b. 1973
   c. 1983
   d. 1993

8. The ACA Code of Ethics can be updated from time to time to reflect changes in the field. True or false?

    a. True

    b. False

9. The 1958 National Defense Education Act was instrumental to the field of counseling because it did what?

    a. Drafted more civilians into the military

    b. Provided federal funding dollars to support individuals pursuing counseling education

    c. Introduced counseling as a subject of study in all public high schools

    d. Spearheaded marketing campaigns focused on getting the public to go to counselors in their communities

10. Claudia is coming to counseling for the first time. She meets her counselor, Susan, and Susan tells her what she can expect from treatment. Claudia says that she understands the process of counseling, as well as the risks, and that she is excited to begin. Susan makes a note of their discussion and begins her assessment. Has Susan satisfied the informed consent requirement, and why or why not?

    a. Yes. Susan discussed the process and risks of counseling, and the client agreed.

    b. No. Susan didn't ask Claudia if she understood everything fully.

    c. No. Susan did not have Claudia sign a consent form.

    d. Yes. Susan made a note that Claudia agreed as part of her documentation.

11. Susan has been seeing a client, Christine, for about six months. Christine has three young children and a previous drug addiction. Susan suspects that Christine may be using again and decides to confront her at their session. When Christine arrives, she appears to be under the influence, and she has her two-year-old with her. Susan also notices that the two-year-old is covered in bruises. When she comments on the bruises, Christine becomes defensive. Christine has disclosed in the past that she sometimes gets so angry at her small children that she feels like she could beat them, but that she never would. What is the ethical concern?

    a. Christine has disclosed past drug abuse and violent thoughts toward her children. Susan now suspects both are occurring, but would have to break confidentiality to report her suspicions.

    b. Christine may be on drugs again, but she's already been defensive with Susan, so it will be difficult for Susan to bring it up without damaging their relationship.

    c. Christine has made disclosures in the past regarding drug use and also seems to need childcare so she can go to therapy. Susan knows a good babysitter who can help, but also knows that would be establishing a dual relationship.

    d. Christine seems to be neglecting her children. Christine could possibly use education about parenting issues. Susan isn't sure if Christine would be open to a referral for parenting classes.

12. Client information is protected by confidentiality. However, in the instance where a client makes a threat against another individual during treatment, the social worker is required to warn the individual, thus breaking confidentiality. What court case established the duty to warn?

    a. Tarasoff vs. Regents of University of California

    b. Regents of University of California vs. Bakke

    c. Blonder-Tongue vs. University of Illinois

    d. Fisher vs. University of Texas

13. When required by law to disclose confidential information about a client, the counselor should always discuss the disclosure with the client before the disclosure occurs. Is this true or false? Why?

a. False. At the time of the informed consent, the client should have been told about legal requirements that cause the counselor to break confidentiality, and therefore, the counselor never needs to discuss a specific disclosure with the client.

b. True. The counselor has to get the client to sign a new informed consent form stating that the client understands the disclosure will be made.

c. False. The counselor should assess any threat to their personal safety, or the safety of others, and should only discuss the disclosure with the client if no one appears to be at risk of harm.

d. True. The counselor has a duty to tell the client that a disclosure is being made and that confidentiality is being broken.

14. Counselors strive to consider cultural impact on individual values. How should cultural differences and values be addressed?

a. Cultural values and differences should be pointed out so that the client knows the counselor is aware of them.

b. Cultural values and differences should be learned by the counselor and worked around when issues arise.

c. Cultural values and differences should be learned by the counselor and used as strengths and to empower change.

d. Cultural values and differences should be compared to the greater society to find similarities.

15. At every level of professional development, it is important to continually participate in education opportunities. Why is this important to the values of counseling?

a. Continuing education is necessary in order to maintain a level of competence in the area of expertise that the counselor practices.

b. Continuing education is required to maintain licensure, and licensure ensures that the counselor is regarded as a capable professional.

c. Conferences and learning situations provide networking opportunities that can aid in interdisciplinary collaboration.

d. Education is an ongoing personal journey.

Answer Explanations

1. D: Counseling is a diverse field and practitioners can work in a number of different settings, including all of the ones listed. Therefore, *All of the above* is the correct answer.

2. C: Carl Rogers was responsible for developing and influencing many of the theories related to understanding humans holistically. Choice *A*, Wilhelm Wundt, was a German physician who founded the Institute of Experimental Psychology. Choice *B*, Sigmund Freud, is considered the founder of psychoanalysis. Choice *D*, Raymond Cattell, is known for his exploration into empirical psychology and is known for developing theories on fluid and crystallized intelligence.

3. B: The United States Department of Veterans Affairs helped expand services after World War II in order to help returning servicemen transition back into civilian life and civilian workforce.

4. A: When working with counseling clients online, you must encrypt all client intake information, communication, evaluations, and other related records. Encryption works by securing messages sent online so that only the sender and the target audience are able to see the information. Choices *B, C,* and *D* won't help maintain the client's privacy.

5. C: The term nonmaleficence means "do no harm" and is often used in ethical contexts. Choice *A*, nonhomogeneity, means composition from like parts, and does not make sense in this context. Choice *B*, nonmalignant, is a word used to describe something that is threatening to health or life. Choice *D*, nonchalance, is the state of appearing relaxed and calm.

6. A: The World Health Organization publishes the International Classification of Diseases (ICD) as an international resource for medical and epidemiological data, health statuses, and other health information. The United Nations, Choice *B*, is a global union of members dedicated to confronting, managing, and solving world problems. The International Journal of Health Sciences, Choice *C*, is a peer-reviewed journal dedicated to all aspects of health. The United States Agency for International Development, Choice *D*, administers civilian foreign aid when needed.

7. C: In 1983, the ACA launched the National Board for Certified Counselors. The establishment of this credential was key in defining fundamental standards for the counseling profession.

8. A: True. The most recent version of the ACA Code of Ethics can be found on the ACA website. The ACA website (www.counseling.org) is considered the most up-to-date and comprehensive resource for counselors, and contains the most recent revisions to the profession's Code of Ethics.

9. B: The 1958 National Defense Education Act provided federal funding dollars to support individuals pursuing counseling education. This support came in the form of federal grants and loans and allowed students interested in the profession to pursue higher education in the field.

10. C: No, informed consent has not been satisfied. Susan did not have a document outlining what counseling would entail, including the risks and limitations. She also did not have Claudia sign such a document to become part of the chart. Documentation of informed consent protects both the client and the social worker.

11. A: Susan has knowledge that Christine has a history of drug abuse. Christine has shown signs of possible relapse. Susan also has safety concerns for Christine's children based on what she has seen and the way Christine has behaved. Due to her concerns, Susan must refer to the NCC code of ethics handbook that says serious harm to another individual must be revealed. Susan will be required to break confidentiality in this situation.

12. A: Tarasoff vs. Regents of University of California is the correct answer. In this 1976 case, the therapist failed to notify the intended victim of the threat of harm. After the client had stopped seeking treatment, he then attacked and killed Tarasoff, prompting her family to sue the University and therefore establishing the duty to warn. None of the other cases directly relate to duty to warn.

13. C: False. A counselor should always assess their own personal safety, as well as the safety of others, when deciding if a confidential disclosure should be discussed with the client. For example, a counselor is working with someone who has a history of violence toward women, and he discloses that he has been contemplating harming his neighbor who has turned down his advances. In this instance, it would be safer if the counselor didn't discuss the disclosure with the client. Given his history of violence, discussing the disclosure might put both the counselor and the neighbor at risk.

14. C: Cultural values and beliefs should be researched and learned when working with clients from a different culture. These values should then be used as strengths during goal development to aid the client in making the changes they desire.

15. A: Competence is the reason that counselors need to be continually educated. This is important so that the social worker can provide the services in which they are trained and remain up-to-date on research and practice.

Dear NCE Test Taker,

We would like to start by thanking you for purchasing this study guide for your NCE exam. We hope that we exceeded your expectations.

Our goal in creating this study guide was to cover all of the topics that you will see on the test. We also strove to make our practice questions as similar as possible to what you will encounter on test day. With that being said, if you found something that you feel was not up to your standards, please send us an email and let us know.

We would also like to let you know about another book in our catalog that may interest you.

NCMHCE

This can be found on Amazon: amazon.com/dp/1628455071

We have study guides in a wide variety of fields. If the one you are looking for isn't listed above, then try searching for it on Amazon or send us an email.

Thanks Again and Happy Testing!
Product Development Team
info@studyguideteam.com

Interested in buying more than 10 copies of our product? Contact us about bulk discounts:

bulkorders@studyguideteam.com